Praise for
Walk On

"If you've ever felt like throwing a red flag on God because it looked like He made the wrong call in your life, Ben's story will give you hope—and show you that God has a game plan and purpose for you that's far better than you could ever imagine."

—Dr. Tony Evans, pastor of Oak Cliff Bible Fellowship and founder of the Urban Alternative

"An amazing story from an amazing person. Ben's story shows that hard work and an open mind can lead to a wonderful journey."

—Steve Kerr, head coach for the Golden State Warriors

"God delights in doing mighty things through unlikely leaders. We see this over and over in Scripture, and we witness it firsthand in Ben Malcolmson's life. Overcoming great odds and pursuing his God-given dreams, Ben has become a high-impact leader and influencer. He has my deepest respect, and after you read this book, I'm sure he'll have yours as well."

—Mark Batterson, *New York Times* best-selling author of *Whisper* and lead pastor of National Community Church

"There are numerous ways a person gets into football, and many walk-on stories, but none quite like Ben Malcolmson's. Inspirational, encouraging, and a wonderful example of trusting God's plan."

—Russell Wilson, Super Bowl–winning quarterback for the Seattle Seahawks

"*There must be more.* This simple phrase most often finds its way into the depths of our hearts in the quiet moments after our perceived greatest victories or lowest defeats. There is no greater encouragement in seeking the answer than to know we are not alone in this journey. Ben's story will let you know you are not alone and help you find your True North. Seeking God's plan for your life? Take this journey and . . . *walk on!*"

—SHANE WILLIAMSON, president and CEO of the
Fellowship of Christian Athletes

"*Walk On* is an inspiring story that encourages all of us to live boldly and maximize the opportunities God gives us."

—ANDREW CATHY, senior vice president of Chick-fil-A Inc.

"As a lifelong sports fan (and a decade-long Ben Malcolmson fan), I'm a sucker for an underdog story. What makes *Walk On* so captivating is not just the odds Ben overcame or even the incredible drive he had to overcome them, but that he made his journey all about people and cultivating deep, self-sacrificial relationships. Call it unconventional, call it divine; Ben's story will motivate, challenge, and compel you to dream bigger than you think you're capable of and to love people well along the way."

—SAMANTHA PONDER, ESPN "Sunday NFL
Countdown" host

"Ben Malcolmson's compelling tale of the ups and downs in the life of a young athlete rings so true you won't be able to put it down. Why? Because *Walk On* is Ben's true story. As you travel with him from high school to college to the NFL, Ben shares the struggles and victories that tested and affirmed his growing faith. Personal challenges and Bible quotes after every chapter bring the book's message directly into your daily life. I hope you read *Walk On*—and pass it along to someone you care about."

—KEN BLANCHARD, coauthor of *The New One Minute Manager* and *Servant Leadership in Action*

"In *Walk On,* Ben Malcolmson not only shares the bright spots of his personal journey that has now landed him beside one of the NFL's most respected coaches, but he also shares the bleak, sometimes painful moments that helped him focus on a life of purpose. His story is genuine—just like Ben—and comes from such a heartfelt place that it's sure to capture the attention of those wondering what it looks like to live a life that follows Jesus."

—JUDAH SMITH, lead pastor of Churchome and *New York Times* best-selling author of *Jesus is _____.*

"Dedication is a characteristic attributed to passionate athletes. Ben is dedicated and passionate about football, but he's even more dedicated and passionate about following God and serving His people. I would encourage everyone to read Ben's story. And the best part of it all is that Ben isn't done!"

—CHAD VEACH, lead pastor of Zoe Church and author of *Faith Forward Future*

"We often get so caught up in our own plans of life and weathering the ups and downs that we forget what it all comes back to. Ben's story shows us that God's timing and desires for our lives are bigger and greater than ours are. And as amazing as it is to travel with Ben through these pages all the way to the Super Bowl, he reminds us that the journey is also just as important as the destination. It is the beauty of how God weaves every step, disappointment, opportunity, and person we encounter together to be even greater than we could ever imagine."

—Bo Rinehart, NEEDTOBREATHE

"Even if you don't know much about football, you're really going to enjoy this book. It's full of heart, but that's not what makes it good. *Walk On* reminds us how God can turn our worst moments into our best ones, make our biggest setbacks our greatest gains, and to live fully, love generously, and leave it all on the field."

—Maria Goff, best-selling author of *Love Lives Here*

"*Walk On* will renew your faith in a God who moves in the hearts of His people—people like you and me—to accomplish His unfathomable purposes."

—Miles McPherson, former NFL player, author of *Do Something: Make Your Life Count,* and lead pastor of Rock Church

WALK ON

From Pee Wee Dropout
to the NFL Sidelines—
My Unlikely Story of
Football, Purpose, and
Following an Amazing God

FOREWORD BY PETE CARROLL

BEN MALCOLMSON

WITH PATTI MCCORD

MULTNOMAH

WALK ON

All Scripture quotations, unless otherwise indicated, are taken from the Holy Bible, New Living Translation, copyright © 1996, 2004, 2007, 2013, 2015 by Tyndale House Foundation. Used by permission of Tyndale House Publishers Inc., Carol Stream, Illinois 60188. All rights reserved. Scripture quotations marked (BSB) are taken from the Holy Bible, Berean Study Bible, BSB copyright ©2016 by Bible Hub. Used by permission. All rights reserved worldwide. Scripture quotations marked (ESV) are taken from the Holy Bible, English Standard Version, ESV® Text Edition® (2016), copyright © 2001 by Crossway Bibles, a publishing ministry of Good News Publishers. All rights reserved. Scripture quotations marked (NIV) are taken from the Holy Bible, New International Version®, NIV®. Copyright © 1973, 1978, 1984, 2011 by Biblica Inc.® Used by permission. All rights reserved worldwide.

For the sake of narrative flow, some time lines have been condensed or modified.

Trade Paperback ISBN 978-0-7352-9127-0
eBook ISBN 978-0-7352-9128-7

Cover design by Mark D. Ford; cover photo by Lara Gale

Published in the United States by Multnomah, an imprint of the Crown Publishing Group, a division of Penguin Random House LLC, New York.

MULTNOMAH® and its mountain colophon are registered trademarks of Penguin Random House LLC.

The Cataloging-in-Publication Data is on file with the Library of Congress.

Printed in the United States of America
2018—First Edition

10 9 8 7 6 5 4 3 2 1

SPECIAL SALES
Most Multnomah books are available at special quantity discounts when purchased in bulk by corporations, organizations, and special-interest groups. Custom imprinting or excerpting can also be done to fit special needs. For information, please email special marketscms@penguinrandomhouse.com or call 1-800-603-7051.

Dedicated to anyone who
ever wonders what exactly
God is up to.

Contents

Foreword

Ben Malcolmson has a fascinating and inspiring story to share that has touched my life, my family, and my career in ways I could never have imagined. He will share the details of his incredible story in this book, and I'm proud to share my version of this treasured relationship, one impacting my life and the work that has surrounded coaching football at the University of Southern California and for the Seattle Seahawks.

My first informal interaction with Ben happened in 2003 when he was an undergraduate journalism student working for USC's *Daily Trojan,* the campus newspaper. Although my early impression of him as a sports journalist was subtle, he was soon to make a breakthrough that would be career changing for both of us.

In the springtime of each school year, leading into spring football, the USC coaches would hold an open workout for students on campus. The candidates who showed up were young wide-eyed types with high hopes and big dreams of playing for the USC Trojans! The coaches took these workouts very seriously in their search for potential nonscholarship walk-on athletes. We wanted to create an opportunity for students to make a dream come true.

Having a role in the lives of these players as they pursued their dreams of playing big-time college football was something I always held dear to my heart. Most likely the players' greatest memories were of making it onto the game field at the historic Los Angeles Memorial Coliseum—and fittingly so. But for me, knowing they got to pull on that helmet and wear the cardinal and gold was everything. To share the challenges and excitement of representing that great program has been a lifelong treasure.

In March 2006, Ben approached me with a wild thought. He wanted to try out for Trojan football and write about the experience for a *Daily Trojan* article. He was excited about the idea, and finding no real objections, I gave it a green light. That was the beginning of the relationship that would forever impact my days to follow.

As for the workout, Ben was athletic and demonstrated basic ball-catching skills. Based on the less-than-stellar competition, the uniqueness of what he offered made it happen. Ben was invited to join the USC Trojan football team! There had been a long-standing, proud tradition of USC walk-on football players, and Ben became part of that select group.

Ben established himself as a hardworking, dedicated ballplayer, and when he was challenged with a devastating shoulder injury and a daunting rehabilitation, he showed his true character and competitiveness. He eventually overcame the rigorous rehab and made it to the playing field prior to graduation.

After graduating, Ben was offered and accepted an internship in my office. Giving him an opportunity to continue to help the Trojans may have been one of the most significant decisions of my working life. He found himself situated in the jam-packed outer office with only enough room for a keyboard and a computer screen, but from that postage-stamp spot, Ben began a career in football and in the new, wide-open frontier of the soon-to-flourish intersection of sports and social media.

Ben worked with me on a moment-to-moment exchange to formulate the brand that was the Trojan football program. He also helped create a line of communication outside traditional media that allowed us to directly share our Trojan football programming and messaging with the fans. We created the USC *Ripsit* blog that was, at the time, a forerunner and trendsetter.

Not long after that, Ben got my attention with a suggestion of another new mode we might consider experimenting with—Twitter! Two-million-plus (and still counting) followers later, it's obvious that again Ben was ahead of the curve.

Throughout our time together Ben has demonstrated unmatched dedication, loyalty, innovation, and friendship. In 2010, when I came to the Seattle Seahawks, I asked Ben to come with me and continue our work. His creativity and innovation are evident every day in all that we do here in Seattle.

These last eleven-plus years together at USC and the Seahawks have been full of great challenges, thrills, and excitement. We have crossed paths with so many extraordinary people from players and coaches to administrators, fans, celebrities, and statesmen. Former Heisman Trophy winners and future Hall of Famers have all left their marks on an unforgettable run.

Throughout all the savored victories and heartbreaking defeats, there has been no one person who has been more integrally involved with and contributed more to my work than Ben.

Pete Carroll

Super Bowl Stunner

The Super Bowl was on the line, and I had a feeling I would remember the next thirty seconds for the rest of my life.

My eyes were on my boss, Seattle Seahawks head coach Pete Carroll, frantically pacing in front of me, chewing a wad of pink Bubble Yum. Even in the incredible noise of the crowd, I could almost hear Coach's brain whirring. As far as what he was thinking, no one really knew, which was what made Coach Carroll, well, Coach Carroll.

As his special assistant for the previous seven seasons at that point, my job at the end of every game was to craft a bullet-point outline for his postgame speech, and I was already formulating how the key themes would lay out, since it seemed obvious the Seattle Seahawks were on their way to a second straight Super Bowl win. Down by 4 points, second down on the 1-yard line, and twenty-six seconds to go, we simply needed to advance the ball a distance I could easily cover with one giant step to secure the game-clinching touchdown and claim back-to-back championships.

Typically I would have been in the locker room by now, roughing out Coach's speech, but there was no way I was going to miss the end of Super Bowl 49 and the chance to celebrate as the navy and neon green confetti rained down to blanket the field, exactly what we had experienced just one year earlier at Super Bowl 48.

Every person in University of Phoenix Stadium on that cool February night had risen to their feet as the anticipation quickly built to a crescendo, the sound of the crowd a near-deafening roar, a cacophony. Circling the field was a sea of media personalities, security personnel, and photographers jockeying for position to get the perfect shot when we crossed the goal line and won the game.

With my journalism background, I had been trained to always anticipate the ending of a story before it happened so I could get a head start on writing it. The story lines of this particular postgame speech were going to be magical: the defending champion Seahawks had won eight consecutive games to reach Super Bowl 49 and now stood on the precipice of history. Winning one Super Bowl is an incredible achievement, but winning back-to-back Super Bowls is nearly impossible. Only seven teams have ever done it in the history of the game. At that time, we were moments from stepping into the pages of the NFL record books, and the weight of that was monumental.

Coach Carroll knew what the Patriots were expecting. In fact, the whole world knew where the ball was going: right into the hands of running back Marshawn Lynch. Why not? The Seahawks had been the most efficient rushing team in the NFL for five straight seasons, and up to that point in the game, Lynch had run the ball twenty-four times and gained at least one yard on twenty-two of those carries. It was a no-brainer, right?

I watched the orange fluorescent numbers on the scoreboard clock steadily tick down with less than thirty seconds to go. The pressure building in my head from the anticipation was bordering on painful. *Snap the ball already and take it in! Let's go!* I had no doubt as to the outcome; I simply wanted to get it over with so we would be Super Bowl champs once again.

I couldn't hear the snap count in the roar of the stadium, but the ball passed perfectly from the center into Russell Wilson's ready hands. With smooth poise, he took three measured steps backward, scanned the field, and cocked his throwing arm to fire the winning touchdown pass, which would smack wide receiver Ricardo Lockette squarely in the center of his navy jersey.

But as they say, the rest is history.

In a split second, I saw Patriots cornerback Malcolm Butler angle in from the right and obscure Lockette. As the two men merged into one before you could say "Lombardi," the silver and white image blurred, and I experienced one of those moments when you can't believe what just happened and your heart stops beating.

The stadium erupted with a muddled sound I had never heard before and will probably never hear again. As the gasps from the Seahawks fans mixed with the cheers of the New England Patriots fans, I stared blankly ahead in horror. I had imagined a hundred different ways the game would end, but not one of them looked like this. This was beyond belief. While my mind frantically searched for an explanation, I looked back and forth from the officials to the coaches, reading the agony etched on their faces.

Wait! This has to be a mistake. There must have been a penalty. It can't end this way.

It was one of those situations where you long to have the last few seconds of your life back, like when you get a speeding ticket or impulsively spout off something foolish or hurtful and desperately wish you could get a do-over.

The pain of that moment was crippling, as if Muhammad Ali had just hit me with a brutal gut punch. It nearly dropped me to my knees, and I could hardly breathe.

I searched the sideline, where everyone seemed to be frozen in time, until I saw Coach Carroll, slumped forward, elbows on his knees with his head bowed, his hands clasped in front of him, and his black headset trailing behind him like a sad dog's tail. Seeing him like that was heart wrenching for me. I had an idea what the cost had been to him; he had invested his forty-year coaching career to get to this point. To watch someone who had become like a father to me experience that depth of pain was almost too much to bear.

In a matter of moments, we went from back-to-back Super Bowl champs to losing in the most painful way possible. *Sports Illustrated* dubbed it "the worst play call in NFL history" and *that* play along with *that* game will undoubtedly be remembered by sports fans for a long time.

As the final twenty seconds ran off the clock, I snapped back into work mode, and the instant I saw 0:00, I bolted for the locker room. I mentally tossed my postgame victory speech into the trash can and tried to compose some words of consolation for Coach to deliver in just a few minutes. It didn't take long for the locker room to fill, and I watched a hundred grown men express their grief in a variety of ways. Some were weeping with clenched teeth and tears rolling down their cheeks, while others were pounding their fists into the gray metal lockers.

I know this may sound like a gross overreaction to a football game, but this was what these guys had been working for and sacrificing for their entire lives. We all knew there were no guarantees; many of us would never be there again.

The air was thick, and one question blanketed the room like an Arizona desert sandstorm. It was the exact question being asked by the more than 114 million flabbergasted television viewers: Why in the world would you call *that* play? But this wasn't the time to sketch out Xs and Os on the whiteboard or to debate strategy; that would be an exercise for another day.

When Coach brushed by me, I held out his postgame speech and quietly asked, "Do you want this?" He reached for it without even looking up, but instead of grabbing it, he let it flutter to the floor and stepped over it. It didn't bother me. I understood that the only meaningful words in this moment would have to come from his heart. He plodded to the center of the room, head down, shoulders sagging, while the entire team slowly encircled him. I stepped back and stood just outside the ring of the team, wanting to give the guys their space.

The room was quiet now, and Coach Carroll raised his head as he calmly and resolutely looked at the face of every player in turn. With emotion, while jabbing his index finger into the center of his chest, he said, "If you're going to blame anyone, if you are going to point any fingers, you can point them right here at me. You don't blame anyone else here, any player or any other coach, you . . . blame . . . me. This was completely my fault. I'm sorry, guys."

Right when he said that, I felt the tension that had been building in the room dissipate, and each man went slack with the realization he had just been absolved of any responsibility. Coach Carroll could have blamed a number of different guys or pinned the loss on his assistant coaches, but on behalf of his players and staff, he took the fall.

I had now experienced both ends of football's emotional spectrum—the utter elation of a Super Bowl victory one year before in New York and the tormenting heartbreak of defeat on that crushing night in Arizona.

A painful loss like this, whether in sports or other circumstances, often brings reflection.

I thought back to our Super Bowl championship and remembered how most of us felt let down in the days following. You work your whole life for something, thinking that when you finally achieve it, you will be fulfilled and satisfied; your life will be complete. But that wasn't the case at all. We were sitting in a staff meeting only two days after our Super Bowl 48 win when Coach Carroll asked, "Does this feel as good as you guys thought it was going to feel?" We all agreed that something was missing; there must be more.

I had run this extreme gamut of emotions once before in my life. Eight years earlier I reached a summit by accomplishing something far greater than I ever dreamed possible before falling into a dark valley where I experienced a depth of sorrow that nearly broke me. That journey allowed me to discover the one thing that has changed my life more than any Super Bowl victory ever could.

What follows is my story. And as you read it, I encourage you to think about *your* story—and welcome with great joy the divine nudges that give you hope as you walk on in your faith journey.

Rude Awakening

Had I known the day ahead was going to change the course of my life, I probably would have been more eager to get out of bed that morning.

But for a college student at the University of Southern California, especially a second-semester senior, waking up at 7:30 a.m. felt painful. On that Thursday in March, I made the sacrifice of getting up so early to celebrate my friend Tim's birthday at Denny's across the street from campus. The air was thick with the smell of freshly brewed coffee and hot grease, the universal Denny's smell that sticks to your clothes for the rest of the day.

With USC's spring break just a day away, students were all looking forward to a week off that we would spend on the slopes of Colorado, lounging on a crowded beach in Mexico's Cabo San Lucas, or at home to take advantage of Mom's laundry service. I was going on a road trip with twelve of my buddies to Crested Butte, Colorado, to spend five days skiing without a textbook in sight. While eating my go-to $3.99 Grand Slam, I drifted off in a daydream of knee-deep powder. I was roused back to reality just in time to join a pitiful, off-key rendition of "Happy Birthday" and watch

Tim blow out the blue and white striped candle stuck lopsided in his pancake.

Half an hour later, I hopped on my bike and rode the half mile back to the fraternity house, considering my options for the next couple of hours. Since I didn't have class until eleven, I had some time to pull together my notes and maybe even complete the article I was writing for USC's newspaper, the *Daily Trojan*, about the walk-on football tryouts that had taken place on Tuesday.

As a journalism major and student reporter who had covered the team for the past three years, I wanted a unique first-person angle for the story, so I had secretly participated in the tryouts. I was still so sore that the motions of raising my leg over my bike and pedaling made my quads burn intensely. I thought how dumb it was to have gone through all that just for an article and still be paying for it two days later.

No story was worth that much wear and tear on my body, and I made a mental note not to make that mistake again, even if it was for the article of a lifetime.

At the time, USC was on an unparalleled trajectory in college football history. Two months earlier, the Trojans had come within nineteen seconds of beating the undefeated Texas Longhorns in the Rose Bowl in Pasadena, California, which would have earned an unprecedented third consecutive national title. But even with the gut-wrenching loss, USC had established itself as the premier program of the decade and perhaps even earned a place among the all-time great dynasties in college football history. In the previous four seasons, the Trojans had won thirty-four straight games, two national championships, four Pacific-10 Conference titles, and three Heisman Trophies. Their fans routinely packed the ninety-two-thousand-seat Los Angeles Memorial Coliseum as Coach Pete Carroll spearheaded an un-matched run—all while making USC football fun and becoming the envy of many college football programs in the country.

Unfortunately at that early hour, I didn't have sufficient brain cells awake enough to work on my article. So as the pancakes hit rock bottom, I decided to hustle home and hop right back in my bed, bury my head in my pillow, and sleep for another hour.

After crawling up the wooden ladder onto the top bunk, I collapsed onto my bargain basement IKEA mattress and began drifting in and out of consciousness. I nodded off around 9:30, but at exactly 9:44 a.m., my blissful sleep came to an abrupt end.

Jolted awake by my annoying ringtone—the sound of an old rotary phone ring—I flipped my phone open while trying to focus on the caller ID. "Lana" was the name on the display. *Lana, Lana, Lana. Who is Lana, and why in the world is she calling me in the middle of the night?*

My half-asleep brain struggled to place her until I finally remembered. Lana had crossed my path a bunch over the years, but she had never called me before. I mumbled a groggy "What's up?" and her voice, way too cheery for that time in the morning, said, "Ben! Did you try out for the football team?"

Now I was really confused. I hadn't told anyone that I was doing the undercover tryouts story except for a few friends and the head coach. I figured that one of my friends had told her, and I was a bit embarrassed. I rolled onto my side, propped my head in the palm of my hand, and sheepishly replied, "Yeah, who told you?"

"Well, you made it!" she said enthusiastically.

As if an errant bolt of lightning had just struck me, I was jolted wide awake. "What are you talking about?"

Without missing a beat, she said, "Your name is on the list," emphasizing each word. Suddenly I remembered a passing comment one of my fraternity brothers made the night of the tryouts. He asked me what I would do if I actually did make the team. I had dismissed the notion and hadn't given it another thought, until now.

I weighed a whopping one hundred sixty-five pounds and I hadn't played football since I was ten years old, making this scenario utterly ridiculous—or more like *impossible*. This had to be someone's idea of a prank, and I wasn't particularly amused. I snapped my phone shut without bothering to say goodbye and slid off my bunk onto the floor with a million thoughts running through my head. I knew there had to be some mistake. There was no way it could be real. I bounced around the room for a few seconds like a pinball, trying to figure out what to do next.

I knew the coaches were going to post a list of the guys who made the team that morning, and I had already planned to get over to the football building to interview a couple of the lucky ones for my story. But that call added a fresh sense of urgency, so I snatched my keys off the desk, grabbed my reporter's notebook and pen, and shoved them into my pocket. I looked like a slob, with a severe case of bed head and still wearing the same wrinkled gray T-shirt and black athletic shorts I had slept in. I put on my brown Rainbow sandals, flung the door open, and bounded down the stairs two at a time.

I passed one of my fraternity brothers in the hallway. "Whoa, Ben, what's wrong?" I must have looked distraught, but I didn't even answer. Eyes focused straight ahead, I just kept moving as fast as my stiff, achy, post-tryouts legs would go.

I leaped down the steps into the courtyard, raced to the bike rack, and fumbled with the lock on my bike. My hands were trembling, and I could not get the key into the lock. When it finally clicked into place, I turned the key, ripped the lock off, and yanked my bike out of the rack. I slammed open the back gate, vaulted onto my bike, and tore out into the alley.

It was now 9:48 a.m., precisely four minutes since I had received the phone call. The bike path was jam-packed with students scurrying to their ten o'clock classes. I stood up on the pedals, cranking like I was in the final stage of the Tour de France, and searched for the fastest route through the crowd. My black cruiser bicycle had been my main mode of transportation since I started college almost four years earlier, and we had traveled countless miles together, although none more potentially life changing than this one. My mind was racing as fast as my feet were pedaling.

One thing I knew for sure: there was no way a scrawny, six-foot, 165-pound newspaper reporter, who hadn't played organized football since one horrific youth football experience in the fifth grade, had actually landed a spot on the nation's top-ranked college football team.

This was beyond any sense of reality. Heck, this was beyond any dream. There was just no way this could be true.

WALK ON
Expect the Unexpected

Looking at life with an expectant perspective, through a lens of excitement and anticipation of God's goodness, can fill every day with wonder. Getting that phone call from Lana took me completely by surprise. You just never know what

God has planned for you; it may be something completely
unexpected, far more amazing than you could ever hope or
dream. Will you join me in embracing the adventure God
promises when we live by faith?

> Now all glory to God, who is able, through his
> mighty power at work within us, to accomplish
> infinitely more than we might ask or think.
>
> **—Ephesians 3:20**

2

Are You In?

I knew the only logical explanation was that someone was playing a practical joke on me. But who? Was it one of my buddies or Coach Carroll himself, who had a reputation for being a world-class prankster?

Within the last couple of years, Coach had pulled some whoppers on his team. One involved a mystery guest who arrived at practice in a golf cart wearing a number 85 jersey, then sprinted to the huddle and was instructed to "go long" as a wide receiver. After catching a near-perfect pass, he fell into the end zone amidst Coach's frantic screams of "Don't touch him! Don't touch him!" In a matter of seconds, Will Ferrell jumped to his feet after making his first and only touchdown as a Trojan.

Another of his renowned pranks involved All-American tailback LenDale White. After a staged argument with Coach Carroll, White pretended to get angry, hurled his helmet to the turf while screaming "I quit!" and fumed out of practice. His theatrical quitting of the team was only the beginning of a jaw-dropping stunt that none of the team and staff will ever forget.

As I thought back on those pranks, I became completely convinced that Coach Carroll or one of my buddies had somehow enlisted Lana as a coconspirator. The bike path ended, and I could see the football building, Heritage Hall, just a hundred yards away. I rode my bike full speed into the bike rack, nearly catapulting myself over the handlebars as it thudded to a stop. In four years I had never left my bike unlocked for one simple reason: I knew it would not be there when I returned. But that day I just left it and bolted up the ten concrete steps to Heritage Hall, a stately red-brick building with gigantic arched windows.

Upon reaching the top of the steps, I slowed down, not wanting to draw attention to myself. There, just to the left of the center of the building, was a white piece of paper taped to the glass door. In moments, I was standing there reading: *"The following walk-on athletes will join the USC football program this spring."*

I slowly drew my finger down the names, which were listed in alphabetical order. When I got to *M,* I froze. Right there, sandwiched between Kevin Livermore and Will Mullen, was my name, Ben Malcolmson. I continued, deliberately drawing my finger down to the bottom of the list and then returning to the top, over and over again.

I felt sure my eyes were playing tricks on me. Each time I passed my name, I was certain it would have disappeared. But it was still there, in black and white, every single time. Standing in front of that list on shaky legs, I bent my knees, dropped my head into my hands, closed my eyes, and just kept whispering over and over, "Oh my gosh, oh my gosh, oh my gosh."

I was a student newspaper reporter, for heaven's sake, who thought it would be funny to write an article on the walk-ons from a self-deprecating first-person perspective, chronicling the efforts of the seventy-five hopeful prospects while belittling my own lack of talent. The chances of me actually becoming a bona-fide member of the USC football team were just about as likely as *Sports Illustrated* signing me as a swimsuit model.

In an attempt to calm myself, I turned around with my back to the list and was immediately blinded by the intense morning sun. I squeezed my eyes shut again and told myself, *Ben, relax and stop panting like a madman.* I glanced down and checked my phone. It was 9:58 a.m. To think I had been peacefully asleep just fifteen minutes earlier.

Coach Carroll was the only possible person who could have pulled off this masquerade so flawlessly. I thought back to all the times I had laughed out loud at the poor suckers who were the brunt of Coach's pranks, and I realized I was just about to become one of them. I expected the ESPN cameras to roll out at any moment, while brightly colored confetti dropped from the ceiling and Will Ferrell jumped out from the shadows and burst into laughter, saying, "Dude, you've been punked!" And I would freeze, stare blankly into the bright lights, and look like the biggest fool on the planet.

I was a little ticked off being the butt of this joke, so I decided to get the experience over with as soon as possible in order to salvage the rest of my day. I jerked the door to Heritage Hall open and sprinted up the stairs two at a time to the second floor. I had been there just once before to write my "Day in the Life of Pete Carroll" story eighteen months earlier. During the fifteen hours I shadowed Coach Carroll, I experienced firsthand his larger-than-life persona and watched his executive assistant, Christie Uribe, guard him as if she had been trained by the Secret Service. The football offices at USC were considered hallowed ground, and nobody was dumb enough to barge in without an appointment.

Since I was typically a quiet, behind-the-scenes guy, I had to be much braver than I actually felt at that moment. And it was a good thing I didn't really have time to think about what I was doing, because if I had, I surely would have turned around and run down the stairs even faster than I had run up.

Upon entering the football office, I was immediately greeted by Coach Carroll's executive assistant. "Congratulations, Ben! We're so excited for you!" Christie said. "Let me see if Coach is available to talk with you now."

Oh great, she's in on the prank too, I thought but politely responded, "Thank you. This is crazy!" I was sure she could hear my heart pounding.

Christie returned in a few moments and ushered me into Coach Carroll's office. As I turned the corner, I saw him perched on the edge of his plush red couch, knees spread wide, bouncing a basketball between them. I was dumbstruck, not only because I suddenly found myself in an inner sanctum of sorts—the USC head football coach's office—but also because what was a football coach doing dribbling a basketball anyway?

He was sitting there with a ridiculous grin on his face. "Hey, Ben, what's up?" he asked playfully, his bright-blue eyes twinkling.

As if he had no idea why I was there. As if this was not about to become one of the best days of my life—or one of the worst.

While I was intending to play it cool, I just couldn't think of a way to ease into the conversation, so I blurted out, "Is this for real?" Which was pathetic, but honestly the best thing I could come up with at the time. He didn't respond at first but continued to nonchalantly bounce that basketball and tease me with his silly smirk. The suspense was killing me, and I had to force myself not to lunge across the rug, drop to my knees, and beg, "Please, stop messing with me!"

He was clearly enjoying watching me squirm and finally broke the silence with a tinge of excitement in his voice when he said, "You can run fast; you can catch the ball; we want you on the team." It was as if those words had been delivered via telegraph; it took that long for my brain to receive the message. I searched his face for any indication that he was kidding, fully expecting him to topple off the sofa any minute, laughing hysterically. Instead, he just kept dribbling the basketball.

"Are you in?" he asked. And I knew immediately that he wasn't kidding. This wasn't a prank after all. This was real. "Heck yeah, I'm in!" I said. He finally quit bouncing the ball, chest passed it to me, sprang to his feet, and said, "Well, get going then! It's time to go!"

That's it? I stood there for a moment trembling, while I tried to regroup. I mentally replayed the conversation that had just taken place, which really should not have been all that difficult since it contained fewer than twenty-five words. Coach Pete Carroll, who would eventually be named college football coach of the decade by *Lindy's Sports* magazine, had not only just complimented my football-playing abilities but also confirmed that I was now a member of the country's top-ranked college football team.

I slowly lowered the ball, letting it slide from my fingertips, and listened to the faint *thump, thump, thump* as it rolled to the sofa. I ran my sweaty palms down my thighs and took a deep breath. After covering the team, seeing how the football players were revered, and going through the walk-on tryouts with a talented group of young men who had been waiting half their lives for this opportunity, I understood the magnitude of this moment. This was *big*. For a country music fan, it would be like being asked to play banjo for Tim McGraw, or for an aspiring young politician, like being asked to sit in a cubicle and answer the twenty thousand letters and emails the White House receives each day. It's not like I was going to play a major role on the team, but to just *be* a member of the number one college football team in the country was incredible. To wear that prestigious uniform and run out of the tunnel to the ear-splitting screams of ninety thousand fans was the dream of many. It was the kind of stuff that happened in movies, not in real life.

I was instantly swept up in the excitement of it all and did not give one thought to the practical aspects. As a senior, due to graduate in just two months, I probably should have been thinking about embarking on my postcollege career or at least considering the logistics of staying in school for another year. As an average-sized guy, I should have been thinking about how physically unprepared I was to mix it up with future NFLers. And as a responsible journalist, I should have been thinking about my commitment to the *Daily Trojan*.

But I wasn't thinking about any of those things. Not in that moment.

This was an unexpected chance of a lifetime, and even though I had no idea what I was getting myself into, all I could think about were the possibilities.

In the Bible, 1 Samuel 17 says that to display His power and His might, God chose a young, inexperienced shepherd boy named David with only a sling and a stone to battle a Philistine giant armored in bronze and packing a javelin. And I wondered if He chose me, a skinny newspaper guy with essentially no football experience,

for a similar purpose. And I found myself standing on the precipice
of wonder and the edge of something uncommon, something downright miraculous and truly, utterly amazing.

WALK ON
Strong and Courageous

Do you think I was afraid to walk into Coach Carroll's office
that morning? You bet I was. In fearful moments, it takes a
hefty dose of God-given courage to act on your convictions
and become the person you know you need to be. In what
area of your life can you step out and be courageous today?

> Have I not commanded you? Be strong and
> courageous. Do not be frightened, and do not
> be dismayed, for the LORD your God is with you
> wherever you go.
>
> **—Joshua 1:9, ESV**

3

Floundering

Five years earlier

In the summer of 2001, I was a high school cross-country runner who couldn't run. A dull ache in my hips exploded into a searing pain; I felt as if I had been whacked with a baseball bat. Initially, I thought it might just be the growing pains of a sixteen-year-old boy who, like a clumsy puppy, had legs that were growing every night. So I decided to run through it and tough it out. But within a few days, I could hardly sit in a chair, and just walking across a room caused excruciating pain that radiated from my pelvis all the way down my legs.

The diagnosis: stress fractures in both sides of my pelvis. I was discouraged, and the recovery period of two months nearly crushed my spirit. *It's my junior year in high school, my chance for college cross-country coaches to notice me. What did I do wrong? I thought my extra training was going to make me faster, not destroy my future. Why did God allow this to happen?*

My training and nutrition program had been maniacal, especially for a high school student. I carefully monitored my diet—two scrambled eggs and a toasted English muffin for breakfast, a turkey sandwich on wheat for lunch, and beef with potatoes or chicken with pasta for dinner every night—while meticulously recording every pound I gained or lost on a chart above the bathroom scale. I powered through alternating tempo/distance runs of eight to twelve miles every afternoon, adding a second workout three days a week. I hardly ever went to the movies or stayed up late hanging out with my friends because of my self-imposed strict guidelines for bedtime. My expectations of myself were completely outrageous, and my self-discipline might've been on par with an Olympic athlete's.

The endless hours I spent alone allowed me to retreat into isolation and provided an escape from dealing with the pain and repercussions of my mom's struggles with alcohol. The trials I faced—such as being the last kid waiting to be picked up from practice, muddling through algebra by myself, or looking after my little brother, Clay—forged an overly responsible, independent, successful, and dependable young man who learned to rely solely upon himself for approval and affirmation. With my family situation completely out of my control, I sought to control every other facet of my life.

Though initially I considered my running career to be over, I soon regained perspective and dug in. I applied the same discipline and commitment to my rehab as I had to my training. I went home from school every day at lunch and swam twenty minutes of frenzied laps in our neighbor's pool, shoved a sandwich into my mouth, and hurried back just in time to slip into my seat as the bell rang. I went to the local fitness center every day after school and pushed myself to exhaustion on the elliptical or the stationary bike until I was completely spent and soaked with sweat.

There was no doubt in my mind that I was going to come back

in the very best shape of my life. My dream was to run for a college powerhouse just like my hero, Steve Prefontaine, a legendary runner for the University of Oregon and the USA track team before his tragic death in 1975. A black-and-white poster of Pre breaking the tape without a competitor in sight during the Pac-8 Conference cross-country championships at Hayward Field hung on my bedroom wall. His inspiring quote, "To give anything less than your best is to sacrifice the gift," reminded me of that dream each and every day. However, at the state cross-country meet in the fall, which was my first competition after my injury, I finished 110th out of 115 runners.

While most runners would have been disappointed by that dismal showing, I viewed it as only a minor setback. I believed there was plenty of time to fully recover by track season in the spring. But, while I would not admit it to anyone, a seed of doubt had been planted, and for the first time ever, I considered that some things were out of my control. And the tendencies toward isolation, perfectionism, overachievement, and fear of failure that had taken root in me as a child would continue to grow and escalate in the years to come.

Near the start of my junior year of high school, an unimpressive plain-white business envelope tossed on the kitchen counter caught my eye. It was personally addressed to me, so I pulled it out of the stack and tore it open. Inside was a crisp piece of stationery sharply creased into thirds.

As I unfolded the letter, my eyes were immediately drawn to the stately embossed gold USC logo in the upper left-hand corner. It opened with "Dear Ben" and went on to describe the "Resident Honors Program" for "exceptional high school juniors" who would have the "opportunity to trade a bedroom at home for a dorm room in a campus residence hall, and their senior year of high school for their freshman year of college." They were looking for kids who had a "passion for learning, an insatiable curiosity, and a spirit for adventure." I quickly skipped to the end, where there was one final question that thrilled and terrified me at the same time: "Why stay in high school another year? Get a jump on your life and start your college career now."

As I read through the letter again, I had no idea how or why it had been sent to me. Did my above-average PSAT scores set me apart? Did a high school counselor secretly nominate me? Did they send it to every student with decent grades? Whatever it was, I felt a flutter of hope in my chest. Leaving high school a year early to attend USC just might be the answer to my prayers and allow me to escape the pain and turmoil at home on a more permanent basis. I felt a bit selfish even entertaining the thought of leaving, but my mom's struggles were taking their toll, and any semblance of a family unit had splintered long ago. The four of us rarely did things together, and it felt like we were all on separate paths, moving further apart each day.

Those painful circumstances at home had been pushing me toward independence as a survival tool anyway. Thankfully I wasn't completely alone during my high school years. One day at lunch during my freshman year of high school, I met Shane, a volunteer youth group leader at Highland Park United Methodist Church, who invited my friends and me to attend the youth service at the church on Wednesday nights. Before long I was walking from my house to the church by myself both midweek and Sunday mornings, something I continued to do for the next three years. Shane also invited my friends and me to play golf and grab lunch at McDonald's. Time with Shane was so fun and meaningful because he showed great interest in my life and made time for me. That church family filled an empty place—the one longing for family—and connected me in a new way with my heavenly Father. The belonging they provided filled me with a sense of worth and with the confidence needed to strike out for USC.

I completed the entire USC application on my own, including creating the bare-bones résumé of a sixteen-year-old who had had only one job, at the local bread bakery. I found an envelope, bought a stamp, and dropped the application in the mail without mentioning it much to anyone, except for a few passing remarks to my parents. Even though I knew there was absolutely no chance I would be accepted, I decided it was good practice for the college applications yet to come. I didn't give it a ton of thought after that, but I tucked away a sliver of hope in my heart, just in case.

Two months later, after a church youth group ski trip in Colorado, my flight from Denver landed at Dallas/Fort Worth International Airport on a dreary Monday afternoon. I rested my head on the window and watched the raindrops trickle down in rivulets as we taxied to the gate. I was nursing a post-ski-trip melancholy and hoped I wouldn't have to wait very long for my parents to pick me up. I called my mom to let her know that we had arrived, and when she answered, she immediately said, "You got a letter from USC."

Right then and there, I knew.

No way! I got in!

After getting off the plane, I wove my way through the sea of travelers, shouted a quick "See ya later!" to my buddies, and sprinted out to the car. My mom stepped out to greet me as I hurriedly shoveled my gear into the backseat, and then I dove in headfirst.

With a tentative smile playing on the corners of her mouth, she handed me the letter over the seat back. I snatched it and ripped it open. I unfolded it and was elated to see that glorious gold USC logo. The opening line said, "Congratulations!" I tipped my head back, closed my eyes, threw my arms out to the side, and exclaimed, "I got in!"

My mom was her true self, enthusiastically supportive and very encouraging on the ride home, but my dad applied his logical-reasoning approach and cited all the reasons I shouldn't go. They included "I'm not sure you are mature enough" and "You are going to miss your senior year in high school, which is such a special time."

Nothing he or anyone else could say was going to deter me. As I held that letter in a vise grip, reading it over and over again, I knew without a shadow of a doubt that I was going. My dream of a running career was over but in the blink of an eye, I traded one dream for another. I sent my acceptance back almost immediately amidst my friends' disappointment and my parents' uncertainty. I knew that this was what I was meant to do, and it really didn't matter what anyone else thought. I had been awarded the opportunity of a lifetime: a scholarship to USC and a whole new life. I would never look back.

The next six months passed in a blur as I turned seventeen in May and wrapped up my junior year. I said goodbye to my friends;

we were all still kids, and while they had another year to cheer for the football team, pick a prom date, and don their caps and gowns while dreaming about their futures, mine had already arrived.

On a sweltering August day, my parents helped move me into the dorms at USC. I looked much more like a freshman in high school than a freshman in college. In fact, I could easily have been mistaken as someone's younger brother trailing along to say good-bye. I was only seventeen years old, five foot nine, 151 pounds, with buzzed brown hair, spindly arms and legs, and the muscle mass of my grandma. I was the latest of late bloomers. My dad sent me off with his old electric razor, and even though he didn't show me how to use it, he must have been hopeful that I would need it someday soon. I wasn't quite as optimistic, however, since my face was as smooth as a papaya, with not a hint of peach fuzz in sight.

While many freshmen suffered from severe bouts of homesick-ness, the transition to living without my family was seamless since I had been independent for so many years. While nightly family din-ners, sharing the events of the day, or fun game nights seemed like a mainstay in many families, those were rare for ours. My dad worked late a lot and missed dinner frequently. The occasional family din-ners we did share would typically take a turn for the worse when my mom fell asleep at the table after too many drinks. On the nights my dad wasn't home for dinner, it was every man for himself, and Clay and I often ate on our own. When that happened, I would make myself a macaroni and cheese dinner and retreat to my room to study or watch television. ESPN and *Dateline* fed the budding journalist in me, while *Jeopardy!* appealed to my intellectual side, and I en-joyed the challenge of trying to beat the contestants. *Survivor* spoke to my isolation, and on some level, I identified with their battle for survival.

I loved being in my room as a child. It became my sanctuary where I was insulated from the unpredictability of my mom's erratic behavior. Eating on my own, being alone for hours at a time, and the lack of family activities wasn't particularly depressing to me since I had no idea that wasn't the norm. As the turbulence in my family increased, my protective instincts kicked in, so embracing the independent life of a college guy came easily to me. In many ways, it was all I had ever known.

At the end of my first week as a freshman, I attended my first Trojan football game, a prime-time matchup against Auburn University on Labor Day at the Coliseum. I proudly wore my new cardinal T-shirt from freshman orientation with a giant gold USC logo plastered on the chest. The famed Trojan Marching Band sounded magnificent in person, and the legendary fight song became an echo in my heart that night. Even though I spent every Saturday watching college football on television while I was growing up, I had never seen one second of a USC game and was completely unprepared for the enormity of the experience. The players, the band, the galloping white stallion, the camaraderie, the fans, the noise, and the vibrant colors all made me feel as if I had stepped onto the big screen and was part of a Hollywood movie. This was definitely big-time college football.

As the sun sank in the west and the purplish dusk descended on the field, I surveyed the stadium, top to bottom, awed by the spirit, the energy, the pageantry, and the entire crowd adorned in cardinal and gold. The stadium wasn't anywhere near full, but to see the intensity and the craziness of those rabid fans, you would have thought they were cheering for their team in the Super Bowl. It was all bigger than life, and I had never experienced anything like it.

A few days later, when I went through registration for my classes, I was required to select a major. On the spur of the moment, since I hadn't given it any thought, I declared myself a Spanish major and honestly cannot tell you why. Outside of being from Texas and my affinity for chips and salsa, I had no legitimate reason for selecting Spanish. After taking an international relations class first semester, I decided that it was considerably more interesting than Spanish and switched my major to international relations.

But it wasn't long before I realized I couldn't even find Beirut on a map, nor did I have any interest in what was happening there. By the end of my freshman year, I declared myself "undeclared" and just lived life, doing what I wanted to do, when I wanted to do it: eating corn dogs in the cafeteria, hanging out with friends, shooting hoops, going to class, and playing video games late into the night. I rapidly became an expert at *Madden NFL 2003* and was happy to take on all comers.

Silly dorm shenanigans with my buddy Mark Weaver, who lived in the room next door, also turned into some of my favorite types of entertainment. We'd slide Kraft singles under dorm doors with various goofy and cryptic messages written on their wrappers ("Save the cheese!"), throw watermelons off balconies and watch them splat on the sidewalk below, and see how many saltshakers we could "borrow" from the cafeteria.

As the year wore on, these pastimes held less and less appeal, and I felt increasingly unsettled. For the first time, I began to wrestle with life-shaping questions: *Is this all there is to life? Am I missing something? Was I made for more than this? Do I have a higher call-ing, a bigger purpose?* At that point, I had zero goals and was going nowhere.

I thought back to how I felt when I identified a goal in high school, such as running a sub-4:00 mile. With my competitive na-ture, once I had something to aim for, it was impossible to steer me off course. I remembered crossing the finish line during the district track meet at Mesquite Poteet High School, leaning forward with my hands resting on my knees, chest heaving as my lungs cried out for oxygen. With sweat pooling in my eyes, my vision blurred, and I squinted to make out the bright red numbers illuminated on the black scoreboard—4:39. It was only the spring of my sophomore year, and my lofty goal of running a four-minute mile was on track. At the beginning of my freshman year, I had mapped out the time milestones I needed to reach—freshman year: 4:45; sophomore year: 4:30; junior year: 4:15; senior year: break the 4:00 barrier. I con-trolled all the variables in my life that could make me run faster and devoted myself wholeheartedly to my running.

From my unwavering commitment to running in high school, to my stubborn insistence on attending USC, I had always been driven to achieve and compete to win, even to the point of a self-inflicted injury such as the stress fractures in my pelvis. Now, here I was, with no goals left to conquer. I had taken my foot off the gas and found myself just drifting along in neutral. That feeling was completely foreign to me, and I felt empty and confused.

That summer after my freshman year in college, I worked as a counselor in training at Deerfoot, a Christian wilderness camp for boys in upstate New York. When my mother was in college, she worked at the family camp affiliated with Deerfoot, so starting at the age of eleven, I spent two weeks as a camper there nearly every summer. Nestled in the Adirondack Mountains and bordering Whitaker Lake, it was a gigantic playground, with archery, tetherball, canoeing, sailing, swimming, fishing, and overnight hikes. It was rustic, and I mean *rustic*. We lived in tents and had no showers, no electricity, and no toilets. There were no phones, no televisions, no computers, and no visitors.

We were virtually cut off from the rest of the world. And I thought it was the closest place to heaven I had ever been.

Growing up, I always attended church, but it was that summer at Deerfoot after freshman year when my faith became real and relational. While I had known *about* God since I was very young, I got to *know* God at Deerfoot. As a part of the training to be a counselor, I took a sixty-hour solo experience, a fast from food and the world, with only a sleeping bag, a tarp, a few bottles of water, and my Bible. I stumbled upon a chapter in the New Testament, 1 Corinthians 13, known as the love chapter.

I memorized the entire chapter and hungered for that kind of love. A love described as patient and kind. A love that does not envy, does not boast, and is not proud. A love that does not dishonor others, is not self-seeking or easily angered, and keeps no record of wrongs. A love that never delights in evil but always rejoices with the truth. And a love that always protects, always trusts, always hopes, and always perseveres.

The Creator of life spoke into the depths of my soul, and the message was loud and clear: the way I was designed to live meant receiving His love and in turn loving others. Up to that point, my heart and mind had been centered around me, and I resolved from that day forward that I did not want my life to be that way any longer. The words of that chapter became imprinted upon my heart, and my quest to uncover my purpose was born. During the waning hours of my solo experience, I wondered how exactly that divine revelation would change my life.

As that summer drew to a close, I headed home for a few days to get my wisdom teeth extracted. Without a room to call my own because my parents had moved to a smaller house, I found myself parked on a futon in the living room. Looking like a chipmunk, with ice packs on my jaw and cheeks stuffed with gauze, I sipped on smoothies, slurped up red Jell-O, and savored chocolate ice cream.

I spent the time listening to music on my shiny white iPod. A song by the band Switchfoot titled "This Is Your Life" captured my attention. I listened to the lyrics repeatedly until those haunting and convicting words began to stir something deep in my soul: "This is your life. . . . Are you who you want to be?"

Even at only eighteen years old, I knew I had come up short. After the emerging purposelessness I experienced during freshman year, the eye-opening summer of spiritual awakening, and the realization that I longed for the closeness of a family, I understood that this was a critical juncture in my life, and I began to do some serious soul searching.

Was I content to float along, living for myself, doing what everyone else was doing, frittering away my life on fleeting pleasures? Or did I want to explore an uncommon path, search for a deeper meaning to life, and pursue my God-given purpose? The answer became apparent to me. I knew without a doubt that I was eager to seek, find, and ultimately grab hold of the life God had for me.

WALK ON
This Is Your Life

Are you living the life you truly want to live? The life you're called to live? When I realized how empty my life was, the words of that song spoke to my longings. Those questions eventually hit each of us head-on, and then we have to decide how we will respond. Asking yourself *Am I who I want to be?* is the first step toward discovering who God designed you to be.

> You will know the truth, and the truth will set you free.
>
> —John 8:32

4

The Handshake

In the fall of my sophomore year, I was anxious to begin the quest for my God-given purpose. But it was difficult to stop believing and acting like the only person I could count on was myself. Self-preservation was all I knew. So even though the career center at USC had plenty of resources to help me figure out who I wanted to be, I believed the person most qualified to do that was me.

The best place to begin, I decided, was analyzing what I was good at and enjoyed doing the most. I thought about my favorite teacher, Susan Harvey, who had taught my eighth-grade journalism class at Highland Park Middle School. She managed the middle school newspaper, the *Tribal Tribune,* which was published monthly, and taught me how to harness the power of words.

She treated me as if everything I did were golden, and even if I couldn't recognize the gold inside of me, she would help me chip away until I finally discovered it. Mrs. Harvey and my fellow editors would stay after school in her classroom with the Dixie Chicks' "Wide Open Spaces" blaring from a silver boom box perched on a battered metal file cabinet. We wrote and edited, danced and sang along, "She needs wide open spaces, room to make her big mistakes."

When each edition was finished, Mrs. Harvey gushed over it as if it were worthy of a Pulitzer Prize—and so were we. My first byline appeared in the November 1998 edition, and the article tackled a vitally important topic: the most efficient way to manage the lost and found. I loved the way I felt when I was in that class, and whether it was the subject matter or the teacher who made me feel that way, I can't be sure. Somehow the two became blurred, and my love for writing was born.

Once I decided to explore a writing career, I set out to determine the area of focus that would be the most interesting to me, and not surprisingly that was sports. When I was eight years old and living in Chicago, I started reading the sports section of the *Chicago Tribune* every morning. While other boys my age were engrossed in the comics, I was deciphering box scores, reviewing Michael Jordan's points per game, or analyzing Frank Thomas's batting average.

My family moved to Dallas when I was twelve, and my dad's strongest selling point to get me on board for the move was the superiority of the sports coverage in the *Dallas Morning News*. My love for sports continued to grow as I did, and I might've been the only freshman at USC who had the *Los Angeles Times* delivered to his dorm so he could hear the rustle of the pages and rub the ink between his fingers when he read the sports section every morning.

Armed with fresh enthusiasm after my self-discovery, I found myself at the office of the school newspaper, the *Daily Trojan*. I read the paper every day of my freshman year, quickly skimming through the front sections before diving into the sports section on the back page, where I would read each and every word. One particular morning, I noticed an ad inviting students interested in working at the *Daily Trojan* to attend an informational meeting on a Friday morning at their offices. I had absolutely no writing experience, except for my stint at the *Tribal Tribune* and the one English class I was required to take as a freshman. I did not know anyone who worked for the paper, nor did I have any idea what qualifications were required for the position.

I was worried about my lack of experience but determined to see where this journey might lead. This was my life, as the Switchfoot song said, and a new chance to be who I wanted to be.

The morning of the meeting was unseasonably warm, and since the *Daily Trojan* offices were on the fourth floor of the student union with no air conditioning, I felt like I was back in Texas on a sticky summer day. When that stifling heat collided with my nervous, queasy stomach, I knew I was someplace I did not belong. There I was, a sophomore with minimal journalism experience and without a major, surrounded by seventy-five highly qualified current staff members and budding journalism majors. I was clearly way out of my league.

After a brief welcome, I was directed to the sports office where Jackson DeMos, the sports editor, was seated at his desk. Jackson was a senior with an athletic build, and his short brown hair and five o'clock shadow made him appear more seasoned and older than he actually was. He projected a professional image with his no-nonsense demeanor and collared button-up shirt.

There were about a dozen people clustered around Jackson's desk, and I casually wedged myself into position in the circle, doing my best to blend in. He knew each person by name except me. It took everything in me to muster up the courage to introduce myself. My first inclination, born from my protective instincts, was to turn and run. But somehow, instead of wilting in my weakness, I felt God welling up inside me to provide a strength and courage I did not normally possess.

After the introductions, Jackson went around the group, giving each person an assignment on the spot. As I nervously waited for him to work his way around to me, I wondered what my first assignment would be and feared he might ask me some questions about my experience. Since I was clearly the rookie in the group, I assumed I would be tasked with grunt work in the office or perhaps assisting one of the other staff members. But it didn't matter to me what assignment I was given, since I had an awful lot to learn. This place was a far cry from Mrs. Harvey's eighth-grade classroom.

When it was my turn, Jackson looked directly at me and said, "Ben, you are covering women's volleyball," and immediately moved on, clearly not expecting any response from me. At first, I was thrilled to have received an assignment so quickly. *Wow, what an honor to cover a USC sports team.* But then I realized what he had said. *Excuse me? What sport did you say I'm covering?* I had never seen a volleyball match in my life, which put my knowledge of it somewhere between cricket and synchronized swimming. I couldn't have even told you what color a volleyball was.

Determined to be the best volleyball reporter ever, I immersed myself in the sport and started researching and learning from every resource I could find. Kills, attacks, and spikes sounded more like a medieval battle plan than a sport. I wondered what in the world I had gotten myself into.

The matches took place every Friday and Saturday night in the Lyon Center, a small gym consistently packed to overflowing with a thousand enthusiastic fans who sounded more like five thousand in those close quarters. Most of my weekends were consumed with studying the sport, watching the matches, and writing my articles, and I couldn't have been happier. It didn't take long for me to grow to love the game and appreciate the talent and the women's athleticism. The fast pace and nonstop action—serve, rally, set, kill, *Bang! Bang! Bang!*—made the ninety-minute games fly by. I was all in, giving 100 percent of myself to every assignment and painstakingly writing each article as if it were going in the *New York Times* Sunday edition.

My enthusiasm for proving myself worthy of the role led me to come up with a surefire idea to impress my editor. Since I was a Spanish major briefly during my freshman year, I was a little too confident about my language skills and decided to conduct an interview in Spanish with outside hitter Bibiana Candelas, who hailed from Mexico. As anyone who has studied a foreign language knows, the intellectual ability to read and write the language is worlds away from being able to speak the language fluently. Mercifully, Bibiana spoke impeccable English and saved me further embarrassment.

Each writer in the sports department was required to go into the office one night a week and help Jackson with layout and other administrative tasks. Tuesdays were my night, but one particular Tuesday, Jackson called me into his office and said, "Ben, I need you to cover the football team tonight because our normal reporter isn't available." He swiveled his chair and turned to face his computer.

I'm actually glad he wasn't facing me because my bewilderment must have been written all over my face. I mumbled, "Okay, no problem," and backed out of his office. Once I was out of sight, I could barely contain my excitement. *Wait, did he just say I was going to cover the football team? The Trojans? The number one football team in the country? Coach Pete Carroll and Matt Leinart and Reggie Bush?* This was undoubtedly the coolest assignment in the entire world—and quite possibly the greatest opportunity of my life.

But I was still only a sophomore with barely three weeks of experience covering the women's volleyball team. I knew I had done an excellent job thus far and was honing my reporter skills every day, but this temporary task felt a bit like sending a first-year med-school student to perform open-heart surgery. With only an hour until practice, I found the media guide and gave myself a crash course on the football team. I gradually discovered a quiet confidence, and I sensed this wasn't just another assignment. I was about to step into something extraordinary.

Grabbing my trusty reporter's notebook and a pen, I hustled down to Howard Jones Field, where the football team practiced. I had never been inside before, so walking through the gates and onto the field felt like stepping on holy ground. But there was nothing sacred about the scene before me. There was music blaring, coaches yelling, and guys hitting one another. I was grateful I was going to be safe on the sidelines and not in the middle of the field.

After orienting myself to the layout of the field, I scanned the sideline and located the sports information director, Tim Tessalone. Glancing over at the media clustered around the 50-yard line, I instantly recognized Gary Klein, the USC beat writer for the *Los Angeles Times*. He was tall, wearing black-rimmed glasses, with salt-and-pepper hair. I had been religiously reading his articles since the beginning of freshman year, and he was a celebrity to me. I really didn't want to bother him, and my natural inclination was to hang back and observe from afar. But once again, God filled me with a confidence far greater than I would have had on my own, and I became the person I needed to be just for that moment.

I walked up to him and said, "Mr. Klein, I'm Ben Malcolmson.

It is an honor to meet you. I have been reading your articles for years. It is my first day on the job covering the football team for the *Daily Trojan,* and I would welcome any advice you have for me."

I knew he probably had no desire to converse with a student reporter, and I wouldn't have been a bit surprised if he politely dismissed me. Instead, he was very pleasant and gave me his full attention. Looking me right in the eye, he said, "Ben, the best thing you could do today is to introduce yourself to Coach Carroll before the press briefing begins. Just go shake his hand, and you'll never regret it." I was stunned by this suggestion and had no idea how to respond. I came up with at least a dozen reasons why that was definitely not a good idea. *What? Me? Coach Carroll?* If Gary Klein was a celebrity, Coach Carroll was a superstar, and there was no way I was getting near him.

I did an excellent job hiding my fear as Gary walked me over to the section of the field where the rest of the press was waiting for Coach Carroll. He encouraged me to make my move. "Go for it. You can do it," he said with a giant grin.

I saw Coach Carroll walking toward the media for his press conference, and before I had time to talk myself out of it, I took five steps to intercept him, stuck my hand out, and said, "Hey, Coach Carroll, I'm Ben Malcolmson with the *Daily Trojan.* This is my first day here, and I just wanted to introduce myself." He shook my hand briefly but firmly and responded, "It's nice to meet you." He continued to the bank of microphones to address the barrage of questions from the media crews that included ESPN, CBS, ABC, NBC, the *Orange County Register,* and of course, the *Los Angeles Times.*

I must admit I was a bit starstruck after that handshake and can't remember a thing that was said at my first USC football press conference. After thanking Gary Klein for his support, I was filled with a deep sense of wonder and excitement and practically floated away from the field to write my article.

And it was only a taste of the amazement that was to come.

It has been said that courage is not the absence of fear but the willingness to act in spite of your fear. I would later look back on that moment, when God provided me with the courage to shake Coach Carroll's hand, as a turning point in my life.

WALK ON
The Domino Effect

Acknowledging that you aren't who you want to be is only the beginning. Then it's time to make the changes that will take you in the direction you want to go. The first step is always the hardest. Taking a leap of faith and joining the *Daily Trojan* staff was my first step, and that small step was the beginning of a domino effect that would alter the course of my life. What small step could you take today to start making changes in your life?

> The LORD said to me, "Do not say, 'I am too young.' You must go to everyone I send you to and say whatever I command you. Do not be afraid of them, for I am with you and will rescue you."
>
> —Jeremiah 1:7–8, NIV

5

The Big Promotion

For the rest of the semester, I worked at improving my volleyball knowledge every weekend and covering the football team on Tuesdays. Even though my assignment was to produce only one article each week, I was so enthusiastic, I could have easily written a dozen.

I was having the time of my life. Since I hadn't given any thought to any future aspirations with the paper, I was floored when Mike Cervantes, the new editor in chief, called me into his office near the end of that fall with some big news. I was speechless when Mike asked me, "Ben, what do you think about being the sports editor next semester?"

Up to that moment, the best-case scenario would have been getting a better assignment, like women's basketball or maybe, if I was really lucky, covering the baseball team. I felt like I had done excellent work in my first semester on staff, but I was still a newbie and nowhere near qualified for such a big role. *What do I think? I think this is the craziest, most wonderful, fantastic opportunity ever!* I gratefully accepted the position and found myself just a few days later sitting in the press box instead of the student section for the final home football game of the regular season.

While I had become a decent reporter, it was still only my first semester as a journalism major, and I didn't know how much I didn't know. Taking on this new position with my minimal skill set was similar to asking the holder to switch places with the placekicker and drill the ball through the uprights for an extra point. I was lacking in experience, and the reality of producing a first-class newspaper day after day with a team of student volunteers was sobering. Published five days a week, the award-winning *Daily Trojan* typically featured around twenty pages per edition, contained four sections, and was crafted by a staff of roughly fifty editors and writers. The increased level of attention to detail and razor-thin margin for error I needed as editor required hour upon hour of layout changes, tedious edits, and rewrites. But my stubborn independence, fear of failure, and desire for absolute perfection would drive me to be successful, no matter the cost.

While perfectionism at its best motivates you to reach your goals, at its worst it destroys your self-esteem when you fall short. My perfectionism was so over the top, I remember noticing only one error make it to print during my tenure as sports editor, overseeing close to a thousand articles, which added up to hundreds of thousands of words and punctuation marks, as well as photos. And that one error was a missed period in a caption—one dot smaller than the head of a pin—and it nearly drove me crazy. The chances of anyone detecting that missing period were less than one in a million, but I could not let go of that disappointment for weeks.

When I shared my inner torture with the editor in chief, he shrugged it off. "Dude, don't worry about it; we all make mistakes. Think of all the right things you've done. This is no big deal." I thanked him for his kind words, but I couldn't just slough it off and forgive myself.

That solitary, unnoticed, unimportant mistake drove me to even further isolation.

My perfectionism had been one of the survival tactics I developed during childhood because my mother's behavior was so unpredictable. Being perfect was one of the few things I could control and a surefire way I could gain affirmation from myself since I rarely received any from my parents.

I remember being selected for the sixth grade spelling bee. I was completely consumed with studying and practicing because I wanted to win so badly. Every free moment I had, I studied the official spelling-bee book. I was so into it. When the day of the spelling bee finally arrived, we walked across campus to the high school auditorium. Although no one from my family was in attendance, I remember looking out at all those seats filled with parents and other spectators and being confident that I was going to win. When it was down to the final three competitors, I was given the word *panacea* and I misspelled it. I was crushed as I left the stage. My skinny little body was trembling, shoulders shaking, as I held back the tears. I didn't allow my emotions to surface until I got on the bus, when I completely lost it. I sobbed in the back row for the entire ride home and felt like a complete failure.

And all those years later, that missed period in that one caption stirred up the same feelings.

During my time as editor, my perfectionism compounded the suffocating weight of deadline pressure. I had to get it right the first time because I did not have time to do it over. Relying on my own strength was exhausting. Of course, I had a very capable staff and could have easily delegated more work to them. But my ingrained belief that the only person I could count on to do it right was myself just sucked me dry.

As the semester wore on, I realized how demanding the sports editor's job had become, and when I fell into bed each night, completely spent, I ached with despair at the thought of getting up in just a few hours and doing it all over again. I had never felt so alone.

With every ounce of energy focused on survival, I did not have the strength to recapture the person I wanted to be. Having experienced the camaraderie of brotherhood as well as the personal touch of the Creator during my summers at Deerfoot, I knew what was missing. At camp our days were filled with wilderness activities, Bible study, worship, and lots of childlike fun such as dodge ball and capture-the-flag games. And more importantly, my camp family filled up the empty places of my soul with the faith and hope and encouragement that I hungered for.

With almost no free time as sports editor, I had given up the activities and relationships that nurtured my spirit and were vitally important to me. I was hardly involved in my fraternity and missed all the deep discussions with my brothers around the dinner table as well as the spontaneous get-togethers to play basketball or grab a late-night chalupa at Taco Bell. And I rarely made time to attend church on Sundays or our Monday night worship meetings. Without any replenishment, my spiritual cup rapidly ran dry. I was isolated and bleeding into those empty places in my soul.

From the outside, it looked like I had it all, being the sports editor of the *Daily Trojan* and hobnobbing with all the athletes and coaches. But when I wasn't working, I was studying or sleeping, and a heavy blanket of depression became my constant companion. My life was heading in the wrong direction, with no time for spiritual growth or connection. I felt the darkness closing in.

When my fifteen-week commitment as editor drew to a close at the end of the semester, I was at one of the lowest points in my life. At the beginning of the semester, taking on my new position had felt like a once-in-a-lifetime opportunity. But after spending nearly every waking moment of the entire semester scrambling and struggling, instead of raising my fists in celebration, I dropped to my knees with my head in my hands and heard that haunting melody in the breeze: "Are you who you want to be?" While I was confident I had discovered what I wanted to *do*, the demands of the job caused me to lose who I wanted to *be* along the way. My disappointment was nearly unbearable.

So I pointed my compass back to the one place that could take me to my True North: Deerfoot. While I could have gone home before heading east, I was already so depressed and discouraged, I didn't have the desire or the energy to witness firsthand the corrosive effects my mom's struggles with alcohol were having on my parents' marriage or our family's overall health. Deerfoot had become home to me, and in my fragile state I craved the safety and security of the family I knew would be waiting for me there.

Arriving at Deerfoot three weeks early meant I would be assigned to backbreaking manual labor to prepare the grounds for the onslaught of campers. My first day of work was my nineteenth birthday. Since I had been practically chained to my desk at the *Daily Trojan,* there had been no time for exercise, and I had gotten as soft as the ice cream at the camp store. I certainly was in no shape to swing an ax or wield a shovel. Each night I collapsed, exhausted physically but feeling better mentally and spiritually than I had in a long time. I actually looked forward to getting up and doing it all over again. And as can happen when doing that kind of work, the walls of my heart began to crumble, putting me in the perfect position for God to rebuild me into who He wanted me to be.

That fatigue was totally different from the life-sucking exhaustion I experienced at the *Daily Trojan* when I relied completely on my own strength. At Deerfoot, I learned that God's strength and the community around me could lift the burden of the debilitating stress and crushing expectations that nearly smothered me. There was no fear of isolation here; I didn't have to be perfect or independent or worry about rejection.

Part of my summer staff assignment was to memorize forty verses on God's faithfulness, and as each of those verses began to penetrate my spirit, they became the bricks God used to rebuild me. One of the first and most powerful bricks He laid solidly in the foundation was 2 Timothy 2:13: "If we are faithless, he remains faithful—for he cannot deny himself" (esv). And while I wouldn't say I had been "faithless" over the previous months, I most certainly had not made my faith a priority. Yet He had remained ever faithful, patiently waiting for me to turn to Him. And as the summer wore on, I felt a shift in my spirit as God lifted me out of that valley of despair and renewed my strength.

By summer's end, I truly was a different person. Instead of that beaten-down, worn-out sports editor who arrived at Deerfoot on his nineteenth birthday, I was a new creation, confident that the only way I could truly discover who I wanted to be was by understanding who God wanted me to be.

WALK ON
Our Weakness and God's Strength

When you begin to align your passion with your talents, it is like a gust of wind fills your sails and you immediately pick up speed. But as every sailor will testify, you will eventually run into some stormy seas. As exhilarating as the sports editor position was initially, it soon became apparent that I would need a limitless supply of God's strength to be truly success-ful. Will you tap into God's power today more than ever before?

> [The Lord] said to me, "My grace is suffi-cient for you, for my power is made perfect in weakness." Therefore I will boast all the more gladly about my weaknesses, so that Christ's power may rest on me.
>
> **—2 Corinthians 12:9, NIV**

6

A Day in the Life

My standoff with Coach Carroll lasted only three seconds, but they were the longest three seconds of my life. Before the summer, I would never have had the courage to challenge him like that, but my time at Deerfoot changed me. My confidence in God's direction as I decided who I wanted to be and what I wanted to do was rock solid.

I was looking forward to my new role as editor emeritus, a relatively cushy job covering the football team and getting to pick my assignments. Being paid to go to every home game and travel to away games—while being required to write only one story a week—was a welcome change after the tumultuous previous semester. Thanks to my *Daily Trojan* colleague Arash Markazi putting in a recommendation, I had also been hired as a freelancer for *Sports Illustrated,* covering USC football for its college edition. I was thrilled at the prospect of having an *SI* byline. I felt like I was now a big-time journalist.

I decided my first article of the year would focus on running back Hershel Dennis, who had been removed from practice and suspended indefinitely by Coach Carroll pending an investigation after an off-field incident. I decided it was time to adopt the persona of a hard-hitting reporter and slam Coach Carroll for not kicking the guy off the team. I was looking forward to creating a sensational headline that would quench my thirst for pride and make a name for myself.

While I hadn't thought through very well *what* I was about to do, I had thought through *when* I was going to do it. I knew the media huddle after practice was not the right place to confront him, and besides, I really didn't want to tip off the rest of the reporters to my story angle. Since I knew Coach Carroll's route to and from the practice field, as soon as practice ended, I scooted down the pathway and waited anxiously for him at the door to the locker room.

As the evening transitioned from dusk to darkness, the shadows on the path were beginning to lengthen, and the lights along the pathway were flickering to life. It felt like an eternity until I heard Coach Carroll's footsteps racing toward me, and I was certain he could hear the *thump, thump* of my heart long before he saw me.

I summoned up my courage and with a quivering voice said, "Hey, Coach Carroll, can I ask you a question?" He paused and said, "Yeah, sure, what's up?" I tiptoed around a bit and said, "I just want to ask you about the situation with this investigation surrounding Hershel Dennis." He answered very matter-of-factly, "I'm done talking about it. I just talked about it out there," and jabbed his thumb in the direction of the field. As far as he was concerned, the discussion was over.

At that point, I should have thanked him for his time and walked away. But I was so intent on getting my story, I pressed on. "I kind of want to push you on this. Do you think allowing Hershel to stay on the team promotes that type of behavior?" The three-second silent stalemate that followed seemed to stretch on forever as he stared me down. With his gaze boring through mine, he lambasted me: "I'm not gonna write your story for you. I know exactly what you are pushing for here, and I'm not gonna answer that question."

With that, he turned and was gone. I was left standing in the middle of the path, grateful for the cover of darkness to hide my embarrassment. I had just been totally shut down by a man I respected and admired. I replayed the scene over and over in my mind as I walked home, and I couldn't stop thinking about it for rest of the night.

As I look back, that interaction was actually a really positive step for me. For probably the first time ever, I did not let my lifelong fear of rejection stop me from doing what I felt I needed to do. And in some way, while I knew Coach Carroll didn't like anyone questioning his decisions regarding his players, I think he respected my courage.

So I took the jumpshot and I missed. It really wasn't that big a deal. Life went on. I wrote a different story about how great the football team was going to be that year, and Coach Carroll seemed unfazed by our brief conversation. The transformation I experienced at Deerfoot had given me the ability to step back a bit and see the bigger picture. The shortsighted sports editor who beat himself up for one missing period on one caption had been replaced by a confident, burgeoning reporter.

I was beginning to understand that growth is more important than perfection, and I was finally ready to move forward with a boldness based on the divine assurance that I was exactly where I was meant to be.

The 2004 season opener was against Virginia Tech at FedEx Field in Landover, Maryland. Covering the game was my first time flying across the country on a legitimate business trip, and I took it very seriously. Arriving in the press box, I casually perused the seating chart, hoping to mask my excitement at being seated alongside well-known national reporters from outlets including ESPN and the *New York Times*. I looked dapper in my brown sweater, slacks, and dress shoes—and my brand-new pair of silver, oval, wire-rimmed glasses.

During the summer, I decided that my new position as editor emeritus warranted a fresh look and that a pair of wire-rimmed glasses would allow me to project an older, more professional image. But there really was nothing wrong with my eyesight, so by halftime the bridge of my nose was irritated and my eyes were killing me. I had to take the glasses off for the rest of the game. That was the first and only game I watched wearing my glasses, and I decided that I would have to find another way to look the part that wasn't quite so painful.

I had a deep desire to do something uncommon in my new role, so I started planning a series of participatory journalism articles loosely patterned after another *Sports Illustrated* writer, George Plimpton. Plimpton believed it was not enough to write an article after simply observing and that to get the best story, you needed to experience it firsthand.

So as a complete amateur, Plimpton put his pride (and his body) on the line and pitched to some of baseball's all-star hitters, worked out as a backup quarterback in the NFL, got battered by a professional boxer, trained as a goalie in the NHL, and golfed on the PGA Tour. He was willing to do anything to get his story, even if it meant a smashed bloody nose.

Roughly following Plimpton's lead, I approached the biggest sports figure on the USC campus and asked Coach Carroll if I could shadow him to write an article titled "A Day in the Life of Pete Carroll" during the fall of my junior year. This was quite a big ask, as Coach Carroll never granted this kind of access to anyone in the media. I was a bit hesitant to approach him with my wild idea, especially since our last one-on-one conversation hadn't gone very well. But to my delight, he readily agreed while adding this caveat: "It's not going to be as exciting as you think." My colleagues were envious, especially Gary Klein of the *Los Angeles Times,* who asked me, "How did you get him to agree to that?"

At 7:29 a.m. on Wednesday, September 29, 2004, I met Coach Carroll at his office and followed him throughout his entire day, which was filled with staff meetings, film review and game planning for the upcoming Stanford game, a slew of media interviews, phone calls with recruits, interactions with players, autographs for fans, and of course, football practice.

Through it all, I got the chance to see the real Coach Carroll, who was genuine, enthusiastic, compassionate, and personable. The only thing that didn't really impress me was his singing as he crooned along with the music continually pulsing from his radio, which was tuned to KFOG, a "world classic" rock station from his hometown of San Francisco. It was a nonstop, action-packed day jetting from one place to another while he hollered at me over his shoulder "You coming? Let's go" from the day's beginning to its end at 10:09 p.m.

A few days later, that story sprawled across nearly three full pages in the *Daily Trojan* sports section and created quite the buzz around campus. I became even more proud when I found out that star quarterback Matt Leinart linked to it from his blog.

Not only were things on the upswing for me professionally; life as a member of my fraternity family was incredibly rich. Alpha

Gamma Omega placed me in a community of forty faith-filled men, and the Christ-centered fraternity became instrumental to my development during my time at USC.

Determined not to forget the lessons I learned at Deerfoot, I intentionally carved out time to nourish my spiritual health by hanging out with fraternity brothers I admired, going to church, and fine-tuning that spiritual antenna for God's direction in my life. We spent our Thursday nights handing out water to partygoers on fraternity row to help combat certain activities that are known to dehydrate college students, and we would also make frequent trips to Tijuana, Mexico, to help build houses. We were like a band of brothers. There was a strong culture of discipleship, providing rich mentorship for the youngest members and growth opportunities for the older ones. And perhaps most of all, my time in ΑΓΩ birthed a hunger for purpose and created a thirst to have a life-changing impact on the people around me.

As fraternity elections neared during the fall of junior year, Mark Weaver, my good buddy and partner in crime from the freshman dorms, approached me with what I considered an outlandish idea.

"Hey, Ben, have you thought about running for president?"

"Huh?" I answered.

"You'd be good at it," Mark said. "Everyone really respects you, and you have a lot of charisma."

I agreed to give it some consideration and just three weeks later was elected president with only one campaign promise: to acquire a house for the fraternity, since we were the only fraternity on campus without a physical home. Even though I was just nineteen years old and had absolutely no experience with real estate, landlords, or business and had no negotiating skills, I believed wholeheartedly that

God had given me the dream of the house and that He would use my role as president to make it happen.

But finding a house turned out to be much more difficult than I expected. I essentially ditched school for the first half of the semester as the logistics of researching options, scouring ads, and tracking down every last lead became all-consuming. When I wasn't hunting for a house, I was rallying the guys to pray about and believe in our dream. After investing hundreds of hours in the search only to discover our last lead did not pan out, I became incredibly discouraged, and the roaring fire of conviction I initially felt was now reduced to just a few pitiful embers.

The dream was fading, the guys were giving up, and my fear of failure was lurking. I was so distraught I could barely sleep. One morning when I was at my lowest point, I trudged down 30th Street, headed nowhere in particular. With my hands shoved into the kangaroo pocket of my sweatshirt and my hood yanked over my ears to muffle the noise of traffic, I was nearly swallowed up in a cloud of hopelessness.

God, how could I have gotten this so wrong? Maybe we should just give up.

And suddenly, a Bible verse I learned as a child came to the forefront of my thoughts. "You of little faith, why did you doubt?" (Matthew 14:31, ESV). It wasn't the audible voice of God, but the message was undeniable: *Remain faithful. Stay the course. Don't give up.* Those few moments reenergized and inspired me to continue the search. I went right back to the guys and assured them that we were not going to give up, and I repeatedly told anyone who expressed any doubts, "It's going to happen."

And sure enough, just a few days later, we received an unexpected phone call from our last failed lead, saying that the other prospect had fallen through and the house was ours. I called an emergency meeting for midnight, trying to make it sound as ominous as possible. When I shared the news, the guys went crazy, laughing and shouting in disbelief while we celebrated with a toast of Martinelli's. I rode that wave of elation for several weeks and recounted the story of God's faithfulness to anyone who would listen. Even when it did not look like things were going to work out, God came through and His promises did not fail.

Once the house was taken care of, my next major challenge was making a decision about my two summer employment options. The first was to go back to Deerfoot as a camp counselor, and the second was an internship in the sports department at the *Dallas Morning News,* which was in my hometown and would hopefully set me up for a job when I graduated.

This decision was really a no-brainer. I absolutely, positively had to go back to Deerfoot. Why wouldn't I? It was the place that meant the most to me in the whole world, with the family that had loved, accepted, and encouraged me since I was just a boy.

I turned to my big brother in the fraternity, Tim Braham, for advice, and as we sat on a concrete wall at the entrance to fraternity row late one night, I wrestled with the distinction of a "spiritual" job such as Deerfoot versus a "nonspiritual" job such as the internship at the paper. I thought choosing the "spiritual" job would show I was more serious about my faith, while accepting the *Dallas Morning News* internship would be choosing against God and striking out on a somewhat selfish journey.

"You know, Ben, there's really no such thing as a spiritual job or a nonspiritual job," Tim told me. "God has His hand on everything, and what's most important is your willingness to go where He wants you."

As I walked back to the house on that chilly February night, my decision became crystal clear. While I knew I was saying goodbye to Deerfoot and my childhood, I was on my way to Dallas.

Working for the *Dallas Morning News* was something I'd dreamed about ever since I started religiously reading the paper when I was twelve. Now I was finally going to experience what it was like on the inside and see how a big-time newspaper worked. I was still a rookie by journalism standards, with only two years of experience on staff at the *Daily Trojan*.

On the first day of my internship, office manager Sylvia Curiel met me in the lobby, and I knew I had made the right decision. With bright, sparkly eyes and a broad smile that spread completely across her round face, she sang out, "Welcome! We are so glad you are here." Loved by all for her cheery disposition, Sylvia was the mother hen of the office and found great pleasure in taking care of everything and everyone. She clearly enjoyed making sure her newest chick got off to a good start, and lucky for me, that was only the beginning, as she took me under her wing for the rest of the summer, caring for me like she would a son.

Sylvia soon handed me off to a couple of the sportswriters who were nearly polar opposites of each other. Richard Durrett, assigned as my mentor, was a tall, quiet, lanky guy, very buttoned up in his white long-sleeve shirt as well as his demeanor, with his wire-rimmed glasses perched on his nose. He was the epitome of professionalism and approached every assignment with meticulous detail. Tim Mac-

Mahon, on the other hand, was a stocky, outgoing guy sporting a scraggly goatee and caused a commotion wherever he went. He was the class clown of the office, and it wasn't unusual for him to grab me in a headlock and give me noogies or to tease Richard by calling him "Dicky D" just to get under his skin. Our little back corner was a very fun place to work, and with their desks behind mine, there were all kinds of shenanigans going on behind my back, which typically involved some type of airborne object. Both men would have a great impact on me and my work that summer.

My first day also happened to be my twentieth birthday, and in the middle of that afternoon, Sylvia surprised me and brought the whole office together to celebrate. As the last notes of "Happy Birthday" filled the newsroom, I knew I had found a new family. They made me feel special and celebrated and even gave me an endearing nickname: "Bentern." With each passing day, I grew to love the crew at the *Dallas Morning News* and dared to hope that I could be a member of this family for a very long time.

I was so ambitious and excited about pouring myself into that job, I often worked from eight in the morning to eleven at night, but I was cautious not to become isolated and end up in despair as I had when I was sports editor. I immediately got involved in a Tuesday morning men's Bible study and used the hours I was alone in a much more positive way.

By embracing that time by myself for spiritual growth and connection, I did not fear isolation as I had in the past. I loved the summer evenings in Dallas, after the sun went down but the temperature did not, when I could walk around the neighborhood in my T-shirt and shorts while breaking a light sweat. With the steady chirping of the crickets in the background, I would pray and talk to God.

Throughout the summer, I applied that same mind-set when driving to my assignments, ranging from high school baseball playoff games to amateur golf tournaments to swim meets, by turning off the radio and talking to God mile after mile. Those times alone had a profound impact on me, and I would continue to integrate them into my life long after the summer had ended.

I was having the time of my life too. Being a part of the *Dallas Morning News* was so invigorating and fun, I couldn't imagine being anywhere else. When that summer internship drew to a close, sports editor Bob Yates called me into his office and emphatically stated, "We love what you do, we love your work, and I want you to know we will have a job for you when you graduate." *What a dream!* I truly could spend the rest of my life with this family. Heading back to USC, I reveled in the fact that I wasn't going to have to search for a job after graduation. My future was secure.

I fell back into my routine in the fall, covering the football team at home and traveling to away games just as I did the year before. I flew to New York to cover the Heisman ceremony for the second straight year when yet another Trojan, Reggie Bush, cradled that coveted hunk of bronze. A few days later, I passed the torch to a new fraternity president, as my job was done. We were all settled into the new house, and life was amazing.

On January 4, 2006, I was hired as a freelancer by the *Dallas Morning News* to cover the infamous Rose Bowl game between USC and the Texas Longhorns. The sun nearly stopped in the sky when the Texas Longhorns snapped the Trojans' thirty-four-game win streak and denied them an unprecedented third straight national championship. While surely a tragedy for the Trojan nation, it actually turned out to be a windfall for me. I was one of five writers who contributed to a huge special section in the *Dallas Morning News* for a game that will long be remembered as one of the greatest college games in history. The fact that I was writing for my future employer made that assignment even sweeter.

At the beginning of March, I had a brief trip planned to Dallas to firm up my plans with the paper for starting my job after graduation. I made an appointment with Bob Yates and was really looking forward to seeing Sylvia, Richard, Tim, and the rest of my *Morning News* family. Immediately upon entering Bob's office, I knew something was wrong. He politely asked me about the school year, but his cheerful and warm personality was absent. Looking up from his desk, his eyes were filled with regret as he said, "I have some really unfortunate news; we are downsizing right now and are not going to be able to offer you the job."

I was crushed. I was supposed to be a writer at the *Dallas Morning News*. This was my dream. This was my family. As I flew back to LA, my thoughts were clouded with confusion.

What the heck was I going to do now?

WALK ON
Trustworthy

Through the highs and lows of life, it can be tempting to lean on your own understanding and chart your course based on your circumstances instead of God's direction. Everything lined up perfectly for my job at the *Dallas Morning News*. I was confident I had followed God's direction, I worked hard during my internship, and I was looking forward to joining a new family that I loved. When that was taken from me, I was devastated. In times like that, trust becomes paramount. Will you trust that God has His hand on you and that He has a great plan for your life?

> Trust in the LORD with all your heart;
> do not depend on your own understanding.
> Seek his will in all you do,
> and he will show you which path to take.
>
> **—Proverbs 3:5–6**

7

Designation of a Beneficiary

I was devastated after my trip to Dallas but had work to do on my latest *Daily Trojan* article. So I jumped back into reporter mode to keep my mind off my worries about the future. In early February, I had come up with a brilliant story idea from a true "participatory" standpoint, one I hoped would go down in *Daily Trojan* history as perhaps the most creative sports article ever written.

I had earned a reputation for being a unique writer with different angles, and my "Day in the Life" series garnered a tremendous reception from my readers. The "Day in the Life of Pete Carroll" story was a hit, and so was the article where I ran a workout with the women's cross-country team—and got my butt kicked. I also spent a day as an equipment manager, doing a lifetime's worth of laundry and loving every minute of it, especially because I knew my duties weren't going to last long.

But this latest idea, a story about the players who were attempting to walk on to the famed USC football team, was destined to be my finest one yet. To the best of my knowledge, no reporter had ever written anything like this. I imagined documenting some lucky guy's journey to accomplish his dream of stepping into the legend of USC football and potentially opening the door to an NFL career.

My reasoning was simple. Everyone from *Sports Illustrated* to the *Los Angeles Times* was writing about the hotshots, guys like Reggie Bush and Matt Leinart. No one cared about the guys at the bottom of the roster, the walk-ons.

Anyone who has ever seen the movie *Rudy* has an understanding of the life of a walk-on football player. The story of that undersized, dyslexic, and determined young man who was able to earn a spot on the Notre Dame scout team has inspired audiences around the world.

I knew stories like Rudy's were much more fantasy than reality. While a small handful of players do walk on and are actually given the opportunity to play, there are hundreds who never survive the tryouts. And of those able to survive the tryouts, most are cut in the first thirty days. Those who survive are used as human tackling dummies, sacrificing for the good of a team made up of guys fighting to make it into the NFL.

The walk-ons are interesting animals. Part bull elephant and part pit bull, they try to charge onto the team through the back door and sink their teeth into a roster spot. They must outhit, outrun, and outperform the other walk-on athletes to have any hope of being on the sideline during an actual game. Since USC was the crème de la crème in college football at the time—the Trojans were in the midst of a historic run of seven consecutive Pac-10 Conference titles and seven straight top-four finishes on the Associated Press Top-25 list— the caliber of this class of walk-ons seemed particularly high. Most of them had been standouts in high school or even at the junior college level. The USC coaches had been following these players for several years, and many had come within a whisker of earning a scholarship.

At that time, the team included one particular, very talented walk-on. Coach Carroll would eventually acknowledge that failing to recognize his potential was one of the greatest mistakes of his coaching career. His name was Clay Matthews, the NFL Defensive Player of the Year just four years later for the Green Bay Packers, and he, along with the rest of the Trojans, would be waiting to crush the newest walk-ons who made the team on the first day of practice.

I scheduled some interviews with the handful of walk-ons who were already on the team and was considering how to add some depth to my article when I noticed an ad in the *Daily Trojan* alerting students to the walk-on tryouts that were to take place on March 7. And then a grand idea began to take shape in my mind.

What if I went through the tryouts myself?

It was the second semester of my senior year, and the story would probably be one of my last for the *Daily Trojan*. This would be participatory journalism at its finest, the story of all stories, my pièce de résistance, the crowning jewel in my college journalism career. And it was perfect for me since I especially enjoyed delivering my stories with a self-deprecating flair and wasn't afraid to sacrifice my pride for a good article.

The fact that I was a newspaper reporter coupled with the wacky twist that I hadn't played organized football since the fifth grade was a story line I simply could not pass up. To top it off, I was what one observer jokingly called a "sunflower": all head and no body. Take that sunflower description and contrast it with the Giant Redwood build of the average USC football player, who would weigh between 250 and 300 pounds, and I was a laughingstock in the making.

I thought back to that fateful day nearly three years earlier when I timidly stuck my hand out to introduce myself to Coach Carroll before attending my first press conference. The confidence I gained from that handshake inspired me to follow him for a "Day in the Life" feature, press him on his handling of a player who had gotten in trouble with the law, and now have the gumption to ask him if I could go through tryouts to write a story on the walk-ons. I knew I had to get his approval before embarking on a crazy scheme like this.

I found him running between activities at Heritage Hall. I knew he would not be in sight for long, so I grabbed his attention and blurted out as quickly as I could, "Hey, Coach, can I go through the walk-on tryouts and write a story about it?" He furrowed his brow and looked at me as if it was the oddest question he had ever been asked. With his mind clearly on something else, he responded, "Yeah. It's not going to be very interesting, but you can do it."

Before he thought about it and changed his mind, I quickly said, "If you are giving me permission, I'm going to go for it." Hearing no objection, I hustled down the steps and out of the football building. My crazy story idea was starting to come to life.

The first step in the walk-on tryouts was an informational meeting, which took place on February 19 in Heritage Hall's auditorium. Part trophy showcase and part athletic headquarters, Heritage Hall glows with rich tradition and history. It's filled with Heisman Trophies, national championship trophies, and an unmistakable aura of Trojan glory. I had never been in the auditorium before, and it had a somewhat sacred feeling, almost like a grand cathedral. It was set up like a miniature movie house, with seven rows of plush cardinal-colored theater seats surrounded by vintage 1968 red brick walls decorated with pictures of past Trojan greats and a giant aerial photo of the Los Angeles Memorial Coliseum, USC's home stadium.

I crept in quietly and took a seat in the back left corner, trying to be inconspicuous. To think that some of the greatest football legends had been sitting in these seats before us was awe inspiring. I imagined that I might be seated in the same place as Lofa Tatupu of the Seattle Seahawks, Troy Polamalu of the Pittsburgh Steelers, or even Heisman Trophy winner Carson Palmer, a first-round draft pick of the Cincinnati Bengals.

The mood in the room felt like the first day of school when no one wants to stand out. All the guys were too nervous to talk or be friendly, and the tension was palpable, as if we were all holding our collective breath.

I looked around the room and saw seventy-four very determined young men with a dream finally within reach. Had any of them known what my mission was in being there, they may have been amused or even angry. But as it was, we were mostly oblivious to the others in the room. Eyes soon focused forward, and every head became upright and absolutely still. All seemed to have a solitary thought running through their minds: *What do I have to do to make this football team?*

Dennis Slutak, the director of football operations, led the meeting, which began with instructions for a mountain of paperwork mandated by the NCAA and USC. Slutak was a stocky man with light brown hair in a military crew cut and a deep no-nonsense voice, who was dressed casually in jeans and a white USC polo. His role was to make sure all the logistics of the team ran smoothly, from team travel to academics to meals to walk-on tryouts and everything in between. He was the chief of staff who ran the show behind the scenes.

It took about an hour for us to fill out the forms detailing everything from our athletic history to summer employment and the designation of a beneficiary. I remember thinking that any sport requiring the designation of a beneficiary was probably a good one for me to steer clear of, and I was grateful that I had absolutely no chance of truly needing a beneficiary.

Slutak launched into his canned speech, which he had given dozens of times before. "We only have a limited number of spots on the team, and most of you sitting in this room will never set foot onto the practice field. Those of you who do actually make the team will most likely be cut at the end of the spring." The truth was, the coaches just needed some bodies to serve as veritable tackling dummies in practice before the freshman players arrived on campus that fall.

He droned on, elbows resting on the overhead projector that doubled as a podium. "So the process you are about to go through— the physicals, the paperwork, and not to mention the pain—will probably all be for nothing." But as I gathered up my notebook and my pen and stuffed them into my backpack, I got the sense that no stack of paperwork or gigantic list of mandatory tasks would deter these guys. They would fight for the right to wear that USC jersey until their last breath.

On the other hand, I was happy that my mission was simply to write a story. This meant nothing to me. After all, I was merely the newspaper reporter tasked to fill thirty column inches in the *Daily Trojan* sports section on a Wednesday a few weeks later.

While I knew little about the actual tryouts, I did know that they would include a number of stations that tested physical skills and that the only required piece of equipment was a pair of cleats. Having not touched a pair of football cleats since my horrendous fifth-grade experience with the Hinsdale Falcons outside Chicago eleven years earlier, I located the nearest Sports Authority, just a few miles down the street from the university, and set out to find the cheapest pair of cleats they had. I found my way back to the men's shoe section and sat down to try on the size 11 cleats I had located on the sale rack for $29.95. That was about as much as I was willing to spend since I had every intention of donating them to Goodwill immediately after the tryout.

As I lifted the lid of the orange box and pulled out the first shoe, I hesitated. What was it about seeing these shoes that evoked a sad, visceral response?

I closed my eyes and let my mind drift back to the last time I put on a pair of black rubber football cleats with a white swoosh on the side. In an instant, the painful memories of fifth grade came flooding back. I could hear my dad sternly call out to me from the living room, "Ben, it's time to get ready for football practice." *Practice, ugh; I hate practice.* Each time I stepped on that field, I was secretly afraid I might not live to see another day. I got pushed around and yelled at and rarely left without a new bruise somewhere on my frail ten-year-old body. I began to feel queasy and wondered if perhaps I was coming down with a cold, chicken pox for the second time, or even dysentery, like what happened to the Oregon Trail characters I learned about on that computer game at school.

I had an entire arsenal of stalling techniques stored in my head as a kid. I would rifle through the list, searching for the one that would be most effective when I heard footsteps coming down the hall. As the door swung open, I jumped into my white practice pants and quickly pulled my white number 43 jersey over my head. My dad stood in the doorway, car keys jingling in his hand, and spoke in a clipped voice, "Hurry up, Ben; we need to go. You can't be late."

When he turned and headed back down the hall, I took one final glance at myself in the mirror. My uniform didn't fit right. Even with my pants cinched as tight as possible, they sagged on my hips, and my pads hung loosely on my small shoulders. My helmet wobbled to and fro on my head, and I was sure that one sharp tug on my face mask could rotate it ninety degrees and leave me completely in the dark. For a ten-year-old, I was small—tiny, really. I weighed sixty pounds soaking wet, and my arms and legs were as thin as rails. You could encircle my wrist with your thumb and forefinger, and my ribs stuck out quite noticeably.

I was simply not built to be a football player. Anyone could see that. Except my dad.

I grabbed my black rubber cleats off the floor in the coat closet and hustled out to our dark-blue Honda station wagon. I let my head tip back on the seat and began to battle my emotions the way I did every practice day. I willed myself not to cry. I did not want to cry. But it almost always happened. I could feel it beginning when my lower lip began to quiver and a stifled sob bubbled up from my throat. It wasn't long until my "Please don't make me go to practice" pleadings began.

The answer from the driver's seat was always the same and delivered in the parental life-lesson tone that every kid detests. "Ben, you aren't a quitter. You don't quit something just because you don't like it." Little did I know, his fatherly wisdom would play on repeat for years to come. In addition to his "you aren't a quitter" lectures, my dad also tried to encourage me to stick with football in more practical ways. He would spend countless hours playing catch with me in the park, hoping to build my enthusiasm for the sport and showing me that practice could eventually pay off.

The rest of the car ride was silent except for an occasional hiccup as I tried to pull myself together. The trip felt like an hour, even though in reality it was only fifteen minutes. Upon arrival at the park, I wiped my runny nose on my sleeve one last time and did my best to dry my tears.

A teammate's dad was the coach of the Hinsdale Falcons, and he was mean. He never smiled. Not once. His demeanor reminded me of a grouchy army sergeant. It seemed oddly funny to me, having a youth football coach who hated little kids.

Practice began with a series of drills that seemed fairly harmless, including running, shuffling around cones, and doing a bunch of push-ups, sit-ups, and jumping jacks. Then the coaches put us through tackling and blocking drills, both of which I despised because the last two things I wanted to do were hit and get hit. Most times, when one of those bigger kids was barreling toward me like an oncoming train, I would just duck my head, squeeze my eyes shut, and turn my shoulder toward him, hoping to avoid a head-on collision.

I don't know why I bothered. I usually ended up flat on my back anyway, looking up at the darkening sky and praying the whistle would blow to signal the end of practice. And my attempt to tackle was actually more embarrassing, if that was even possible. I can't remember that I ever actually tackled anybody. I just seemed to spend an awful lot of time on the ground, whether I was the tackler or the helpless victim.

When we practiced plays, I tried to hide on the sideline. I was definitely the only kid on the team who was begging under his breath, "Please *don't* put me in, Coach."

And much like a Little League coach hides his, um, least talented players in right field, our coaches put me at the youth football equivalent: defensive tackle. The job of a real-life defensive tackle is to control an area along the line of scrimmage and make sure no one gets through. A good defensive tackle is quick, strong, and able to get his opponent off balance.

Unfortunately, I was not good at any of those things. If you have ever tried to run through a flimsy cardboard box to crumple it beneath you, you will understand that I played the part of the cardboard box. Instead of crumpling, though, I was most often pummeled to the ground. But I wasn't dumb enough to do that repeatedly. Most times I would just save the lineman the hassle by dropping to the ground before getting hit, just like we learned to do in the duck-and-cover tornado drill at school.

Although I went to great lengths not to be noticed, I didn't need to worry. The coaches were well aware of my lack of football skills and size. When it came to game days, the rules stated that every player must have the opportunity to play at least four snaps. And every game, I could count on playing exactly four snaps.

When that season mercifully ended with a loss in the first round of the playoffs, I made a promise to myself: I would never, ever play football again. Even if I couldn't watch Nickelodeon for a month, even if I had to take out the trash for a year or share my Legos with my brother, I was never, ever going to play football again.

WALK ON
Your Past Doesn't Dictate Your Future

No matter what has happened, your past has no bearing on God's calling for you. My fifth-grade football experience could have been summed up perfectly in two words: *epic fail.* Your pedigree doesn't constrain you, your previous decisions don't define you, and your limitations don't hold you back. Will you leave your past behind and set aside your supposed shortcomings to move forward into the magnificent future God has for you?

> I have not achieved [perfection], but I focus on this one thing: Forgetting the past and looking forward to what lies ahead, I press on to reach the end of the race and receive the heavenly prize for which God, through Christ Jesus, is calling us.
>
> **—Philippians 3:13-14**

8

Wide Receiver?

As the countdown to the tryouts began, I was feeling anxious about being physically prepared and tried to get a handle on my nerves. *What am I so worried about?* There was absolutely nothing at stake here for me. This was just going to be another story among the hundreds I had written up to this point and the thousands more I would write over my lifetime. I finally decided that my nerves were directly related to my pride. *Yes! That's it. I just don't want to embarrass myself in front of the other guys who are trying out or the coaches.*

And most importantly, I did not want to look like a dork in front of Coach Carroll. He had already warned me that this wasn't going to be a very good story. I certainly didn't want to prove him right by collapsing on the field because I couldn't keep up or by doing something dumb like spraining my ankle.

The Tuesday morning of the tryouts dawned a perfect California day—pale-blue sky, seventy-two degrees. The tryouts were scheduled for two o'clock, and I planned to arrive an hour early in hopes of getting some interviews for my story. I was determined to operate under my cloak-and-dagger cover and tell no one I was a reporter. To everyone except Coach Carroll, I was simply another one of the prospects, who happened to have the physique of a scarecrow and was toting a reporter's notebook along with his cleats.

When I arrived at the field, there was a good number of guys already there, working off their nervous energy. Some had their head-phones on, eyes looking off in the distance and grooving to the beat of the music. Some were sitting alone on the grass in the hurdler's stretch, and some were jogging slowly around the field. I thought this would be my first opportunity to gather some good material for my story.

Unfortunately, while most of the guys were polite, they clearly did not want to be disturbed. I got short or one-word answers to my questions, and then they turned away. I desperately wanted to respect their privacy. After all, I was just writing a story. I would be devastated if anything I said or did caused them to break their concentration. For some, this would be the biggest day of their young lives, and I did not want to interfere in any way.

All these guys were "career" football players. I could see it in the way they moved and prepared. Surrounding each of them was that aura of quiet confidence that can only be gained after years of experience. Since I knew from my research that many of them were record setters at their high schools, I was extremely grateful I wasn't there to compete with them. There had been seventy-five guys in attendance at the informational meeting, but there were only forty-two guys present for the actual tryouts. That meant that Slutak's scare tactics had been extremely effective.

We were asked to sign in on a clipboard and indicate which position we were trying out for. I had no idea what to put after my name since the only football experience I had since the fifth grade was an occasional pickup or intramural game, both of which offered only two positions, quarterback and wide receiver. And because I knew I wasn't a quarterback, I chose the other position: wide receiver. And just to cover my bases, I placed a question mark after it: "WR?" (Imagine Ron Burgundy reading it from the teleprompter in a quizzical tone.)

Most of the guys were wearing some type of official-looking football workout clothes and carried duffle bags filled with extra gear, Gatorade, and snacks. I was wearing my favorite navy-blue shorts with red stripes down the sides and a nondescript gray athletic T-shirt. Since I knew this was a once-in-a-lifetime experience, I put on some of my newer white crew socks as a special treat to myself and to make those cheap cleats look a little better. Before the workout got underway, we were told to grab a black practice jersey from the red bucket on the sideline.

Like every good reporter, I never went anywhere without my mini spiral notebook. But I quickly realized that it looked out of place and might give me away, so I stashed it in my sneakers on the sideline.

By now, the coaches were beginning to saunter onto the field. I immediately recognized wide receivers coach Lane Kiffin, quarterbacks coach Steve Sarkisian, and linebackers coach Ken Norton Jr. They were laughing a bit amongst themselves like the cool kids on the playground who were preparing to tease the first graders. I got the distinct impression that they got a kick out of days like this. It was their chance to flex those coaching muscles and take the anxious rookies through their paces to see what they were made of. Finally, Coach Carroll made his grand entrance. As he strode across the field, his persona was clearly larger than life. And the seriousness of what was about to happen began to sink in.

Chris Carlisle, the head strength and conditioning coach, and his assistant, Jamie Yanchar, started things off. Coach Carlisle was a gruff man with a stern demeanor that reminded me of Jack Nicholson in *A Few Good Men*. His face looked like it was chiseled out of granite, and he never smiled as he barked out stretching instructions—"Stay behind the line," "It's not that hard to listen," and "Hang your hams"—between strong, shrill whistle blows. He immediately commanded respect, and he got it. He was the kind of guy you did not want to tick off, especially on that day.

Carlisle and Yanchar began by leading eight lines of players through stretching, short sprints, backpedaling, shuffling, and other drills. All these twentysomething guys puffed their chests up and tried to find a way to stand out from the rest of the pack. They did their best to perform each task to perfection, always jockeying for position at the front of the line.

No one wanted to be in the back of the line—except me. I was just a lucky spectator, and there was no way I was going to tarnish anyone's rising star. In fact, I loved the back. Since I had no idea what I was doing, it gave me a chance to watch everyone go before me so I could at least see the drill and attempt to do it without making a complete fool of myself. I was worried that my lack of experience was beginning to show at the end of what they called "the warm-up," because if this was the warm-up, I was not prepared for the main event. My shirt was soaked with sweat, and I was already winded just from the stretching and jogging. I was thinking about how pathetic it would be if I couldn't even complete the warm-up when we were hustled off to the first station: timed 40-yard sprints.

Up to this point, I had done an excellent job staying under the radar. Everyone was enveloped in his own little world, unaware even of the guy standing next to him. However, I had never done a timed 40-yard dash in my life, and I feared that it might be my undoing. I stuck to my game plan and hung back, carefully analyzing each facet of the stance, the start, and the actual run so as not to embarrass myself when it was my turn. When they called my number, I moved up to the line and assumed what I believed was my best sprinter's stance. With fingertips quivering and legs taut, I lowered my head and waited for the right moment to load and launch.

And right then, my worst fear was realized. One of the coaches surprisingly exclaimed, "Hey, that's the newspaper guy," and I knew my cover was blown. I did my level best to ignore him, frozen in my stance, but it didn't take long for the entire coaching staff to begin cajoling me, hooting and hollering and laughing mercilessly. "The newspaper guy's here! The newspaper guy's here!" they roared. I shrank down, making myself as small as possible, wishing I could somehow melt into the turf, never to be seen again. The teasing continued as someone shouted, "Let's see what he is going to write about now!"

While it had only been a few seconds, I felt I had been poised on that line for hours. When I realized they weren't going to let up, I told myself to go, then took off. Somewhere in that blur of 4.87 seconds, I could distinguish Coach Carroll's encouraging voice above all the others saying, "C'mon, Ben! C'mon, Ben!" The first thing I heard when I lunged past the line was one of the assistant coaches belting out, "Oh, that's pretty good for a newspaper guy!" And then I could hear Coach Carroll's voice once again, congratulating me, "Hey, great job, Ben!"

Since we only got two attempts, I made my way back to the line and waited for my second and final turn. They didn't tell me in that moment what my time was on my first sprint, but I was confident I could do better the second time around. After experiencing it once, I now understood that the stance was important, but the key was that first push-off with your front foot. You really had to explode out of your stance. I could still hear the coaches razzing me, but somehow I was able to tune it out. I felt faster and ran much better, crossing the line to the click of the stopwatch in 4.72 seconds.

I had no time to savor that small success, though. As soon as I slowed to a walk, one of the coaches started berating me for not running to the next station. It was as if the words *newspaper reporter* were in the bull's-eye of a target that was now planted squarely on my chest. I had no place to hide, and I knew they'd all be picking on me for the rest of the tryouts. Coach Carroll must not have told them that my antics were all a ruse to gather material for my story, so I think they got a kick out of the ridiculousness of "the newspaper guy" attempting to walk on. They actually believed I was dumb enough to make a legitimate run at this.

After the 40-yard dash, we moved to another part of the field to perform a series of agility drills that involved sprinting, shuffling, and backpedaling. Players and coaches were packed into a small area, and with every click of the stopwatch, the intensity was ratcheting up as guys realized that time was rapidly running out to make a good impression. Coach Carroll moved throughout the field analyzing and evaluating each player. During one of my high-knee drills, I became keenly aware of his presence when his face was within inches of mine and I could smell his bubble-gum breath. He shouted, "C'mon, Ben, is that all you got?!" Although I didn't have the guts or the extra breath to voice it, I remember thinking, *Yes, pretty much, Coach. I do believe this is all I got.*

The nonstop taunting and halfhearted put-downs by the coaches were intended to rattle us. And in my case, they were definitely working. The mental and verbal teasing was wearing on me, and I began to wonder if I could actually finish the tryouts. I considered drifting to the sideline and slipping out, because finishing had absolutely no bearing on my future. I already had more than enough firsthand research to write my story. The only positive takeaway from my fifth-grade football days was that I was not a quitter, and I was determined to make my dad proud by not quitting.

Thankfully, just as I thought I had reached the breaking point, we were moved on to our third and final station. At that station we were split up according to positions, and I quickly realized that identifying myself as a wide receiver may not have been a good decision. Since there were only five of us in that group, it was going to be impossible for me to hide. One of the coaches picked up the ball, stretched his arm out as he pointed it at the first guy in line, and ordered, "Run a slant." *Oh man,* I thought. *This is it. The charade is over.* Even though I had been the unofficial *Madden NFL 2003* champ of my dorm as a freshman, I had no idea how to run an actual real-life slant.

At the beginning of the drill, I got lucky and tipped a ball with my fingertips; it hung suspended for a split second before I hauled it in. All those times my dad and I played catch in the park as a kid were starting to pay off. The coaches who were running the drill paused, briefly shared some puzzled looks, and then started harassing me again. "Oh man, check out those hands on the newspaper guy" and "Nice route, newspaper boy."

At that point, I'd had it with all the badgering and decided to just let it roll off my back. After all, it wasn't every day a guy got to try out for the USC football team, and I intended to enjoy the rest of it and see if I could get even more for my story. Running the routes was exhausting, but I was feeling more and more comfortable with each one.

On my final route, I stretched out my body as far as it could possibly go, leaped up, snagged a bullet pass with only my left hand, and tumbled to the ground while miraculously securing the ball with my right hand. It seemed fitting that my last catch was my best, and although guys with off-the-chart talent and experience surrounded me, I was proud of my efforts and confident that I was going to write my best article ever.

When the final whistle blew, everyone huddled around Coach Carroll for a short pep talk, and I will never forget his words that day. "If you make it, you'll be treated like you're a part of the team," he said, as he looked at each and every player circled around him. "If you don't make it, it's not a knock on you, since this is one of the best football programs in the country."

He rallied us all together, raised his fist toward the sky, and led us in a "Trojans" chant. And that's when it really hit me, and I felt goose bumps. I had just tried out for the USC football team. I stood amazed and incredibly grateful for the opportunity.

I hurried over to collect my notebook and my pen and started scribbling notes as fast as I possibly could. The other guys were all sitting around in a somewhat sober atmosphere. Each one realized that it was over, good or bad. Success or failure, it was done. All their years of preparing and dreaming would soon be weighed out and measured to see if it had been enough.

Now that everyone knew I was "the newspaper guy," I was free to conduct some informal interviews and get impressions of the tryouts. I asked a couple of guys if I could call them on Thursday or Friday to see if they made the team and get their reactions for my article.

My body began to feel the impact of the workout nearly immediately. My muscles felt like they had been crushed in a vise, and I was nursing a ton of injuries: bruised ribs, a banged-up shoulder, scraped knees, and a nasty bruise that was forming on my right hand. A bottle of ibuprofen and a bag of ice were my constant companions for the rest of the day.

The next night, I had recovered enough to celebrate my survival by dropping in at a pie social hosted by the Pi Beta Phi sorority across the street from my fraternity house. I was standing off to the side of the room, balancing two plates and alternating bites between pumpkin and apple, when Beau, one of my fraternity brothers, approached me.

I hadn't told many people that I was going through the tryouts, but Beau was one of the few in my inner circle who knew. When I paused between bites, he asked, "How did the tryouts go?" I proceeded to tell him the details of the day, including how extraordinary it was and how very blessed I felt to experience it. With his eyes drilling into mine, he playfully asked, "Have you thought about what would happen if you actually made the team?"

I nearly choked on my pie as I threw my head back and blurted out, "Well, I'm not going to!" I realized that thought had never crossed my mind before.

He continued, "Think about it. What if you actually did?"

I stared at him in utter disbelief and answered with full confidence, "That's absolutely impossible. It's like asking, 'What if someone walked up right now and handed you a million dollars?' It's simply not going to happen."

Shortly after that conversation, I decided it was time to head home, perhaps type out a few words for my story, take some more Advil, and plaster my aching muscles with fresh ice. As I hobbled across the street and stared up into the hazy glow of the Los Angeles night sky, I reflected on Beau's question, but just for a brief moment. *What if I actually did make it?*

And just as quickly, that thought vanished, much as the stars do behind the smoggy LA sky, because I knew there was no way that was ever going to happen.

WALK ON
Fearless

Just as I did on the day of the tryouts, we all face uncomfortable and unfamiliar situations in life. We always have a choice: to face our fears and fight through them, or allow them to paralyze us. Where in your life can you make the choice to battle your fears even when you are faced with difficult or unfamiliar circumstances?

> Do not be afraid or discouraged, for the LORD
> will be with
> you; he will neither fail you nor abandon you.
>
> **—Deuteronomy 31:8**

9

Whisper on the Steps

A mere twelve hours later, I walked numbly out of Coach Carroll's office feeling absolutely shell shocked. I could see the sensational headline now—"Skinny Student Reporter Trades Notebook for Playbook"—and instead of being the proud author of that article, I would be its most unlikely subject.

Did that really happen? Am I dreaming? What in the world am I supposed to do now?

Almost immediately I had a sense, an inaudible response to the torrent of questions I was unable to voice, that this was a God thing. I felt I was standing on the edge of something divine. I was convinced there must be a reason for this. It was the only plausible explanation.

Closing my eyes, I pictured the walk-on list taped to the door and remembered a line at the bottom of the page that read, "The next step is for each of you to meet with your position coach, then proceed downstairs to meet with our Head Athletic Trainer." After opening my eyes, I noticed a row of offices to my left, so I headed in that direction and stumbled upon the office of wide receivers coach Lane Kiffin.

Leaning on the doorframe, I attempted to gather my thoughts.

I knew I couldn't just stand there forever, so I mustered up the courage to gently knock on the frame and hesitantly said in a tremulous voice, "Hey, Coach Kiffin, I'm Ben. I tried out and made the team."

Kiffin looked like a younger and taller version of Coach Carroll, with his wavy brown hair tucked in a white visor and black Dri-FIT shirt with the USC logo emblazoned on his chest. He immediately stiffened, and the air grew thick with his take-charge attitude.

I had been around Coach Kiffin enough to know that I didn't want to be around him. When I was writing a story and needed a quote from an offensive coach, I would go to anyone but him to get it. He wore a perpetual frown and seemed to be angry at someone most of the time. Unfortunately, it looked like today was my day. He barely even looked up when he snapped, "This isn't about getting free T-shirts and a ring. This is serious business, and it's going to be a lot of work. Go downstairs and get your equipment. Here's your playbook. Start studying now."

Without rising from his chair and barely even looking at me, he lifted a playbook from the stack on the corner of his desk and held it out in midair. Still standing in the doorway, I took two tentative steps forward, accepted the playbook from his outstretched arm, and made a hasty retreat. *Good grief, I've only been on the team for five minutes and I'm already getting pushed around.*

I should have realized then that this was a harbinger of things to come. Apparently, not everyone was going to be as enthusiastic as Coach Carroll. If I had any hope of attaining my coaches' and teammates' respect, I was going to have to earn it. (It wasn't until many years later that Coach Carroll confirmed that the negative vibe I felt from Coach Kiffin wasn't my imagination. Apparently, he thought having a newspaper reporter on the team was a joke.)

I headed back down the staircase while admiring that white one-inch binder with a color photo of the Coliseum and the words "2006 Spring USC Football Playbook" printed across the bottom. The awesomeness was starting to sink in, and that binder could not have been more valuable to me if it were made of solid gold. Pausing at the first floor, where I entered the building less than twenty minutes before, I glanced down the dark stairway encased in red brick walls.

I had never set foot on those stairs before, since whatever was down there was for athletes only. Even my press credential, which could usually get me anywhere I wanted to go, wasn't enough to gain access to that area. I had always wondered what was down those stairs, and now I was finally going to find out.

The stairway was fairly narrow, making it impossible to pass someone without one person turning sideways. I encountered several athletes from different sports heading up the stairs, and I turned immediately, sucked my stomach in, and plastered myself against the rough, scratchy bricks to give them the right of way. *Who am I to be heading down here? What if someone asks me what I'm doing?*

When I reached the bottom step, I was facing a long hallway lined with metal industrial pipes alongside huge steel I-beams. Tucked in between those pipes and I-beams were bare fluorescent bulbs casting an eerie glow. I felt like I was standing in the middle of an abandoned warehouse, and after peering down that stairway for three years and imagining the world-class sports facility housed beneath my feet, I was a bit disappointed. Compared to the glamour and the glitz of the first and second floors, which housed the glory of USC, this looked like someone forgot to finish the basement.

To the left was a red hallway, and I decided to follow the buzz of activity that was coming from that direction. I heard the *chug, chug, chug* of a large industrial washer, along with the steady hum of a dryer. As I stepped up to the door, I realized immediately that I was standing in the doorway of the equipment room. The mix of smells I encountered was a disgusting combination of bleach, detergent, sweat, and rubber. Along the wall, twelve plain, cardinal-red helmets were hung by their face masks on pegs all in a row, like Christmas stockings lined up along a fireplace.

I probably stood there for thirty seconds trying to talk myself into stepping inside. *This is what Coach Kiffin told me to do. What if someone tells me I shouldn't be here? Maybe the coaches forgot to send the walk-on list down here.* Taking a deep breath, I glanced around and tiptoed into the room. There were several athletes milling around, and no one seemed to know or care that I even existed, which was fine by me. I noticed a portly Latino guy with a bushy mustache and black slicked-back hair bustling around, wearing baggy gray USC sweatpants and a thick gold chain. He looked like the boss. My voice cracked as I said, "Hey, I'm a walk-on for the football team, and I'm supposed to check in with you." *Does he believe me? I don't even think I believe myself.*

Thinking back to the tryouts, I pictured all those guys lined up on the field with hope in their eyes and longing in their hearts for a spot on the team. Some of them probably worked half their lives for this chance and poured out all their dreams on the field. And here I was instead, a skinny, inexperienced guy who wasn't even trying to make the team and didn't know a quick out from a hitch route. I was in way over my head and felt like such an impostor. I wondered if perhaps God had placed me in this unique situation for a special purpose. But I dismissed the thought since I couldn't fathom how

He could use a guy like me on the number one football team in the country.

I recognized several guys from the team as they passed through and got new T-shirts or traded shorts for a different size. It was so weird seeing those guys on the inside after watching them on the field for three years. I had no idea how I was going to make the jump from reporter to teammate since I was quite sure it had never been done before. Even Plimpton wouldn't have been able to pull this off. Something seemed terribly out of place, and I couldn't shake the feeling that it was probably me.

I heard the other guys call the equipment manager Tino, and he finally made his way back over to me. He was all business as he quickly sized me up as a "large" and muttered, "Let me show you your locker." We crossed the hallway, and Tino punched in a code to open the gray metal door with the USC logo and the words "Players Only" on it.

I really wanted to savor the first moment I walked through that door, but there was no time. Tino was off and running. I don't know what I was expecting behind that door, some posh locker room, I suppose, like you see at the Masters golf tournament on television. What I saw was a very utilitarian locker room, with dingy, stained cardinal-red carpet that looked like it had been there for decades and rows upon rows of lockers.

I caught a glimpse of Tino turning and making a beeline for the far back corner, unaware that I was no longer behind him. As I hustled to catch up, I realized what a mess that locker room was. Dirty clothes and stray shoes were tossed haphazardly on the floor, and there was an array of T-shirts and towels draped over the ceiling pipes, hanging like vines in a jungle. I did my best to navigate my way through that maze, hoping to catch up to Tino before he realized I was missing.

My locker was located in a corner where even the scant fluorescent lights barely reached, as far back in the locker room as you could possibly go. Clearly locker assignments reflected your importance to the team, and based on where mine was located, I was just barely a scrub. One more row, and I would be standing in the showers. But I didn't care. Right then, soaking in the afterglow of the enormity of what life had just handed me, I was the happiest scrub on the planet, and that locker was the most beautiful thing I had ever seen. Along the top of most of the lockers was a cardinal nameplate etched with each player's last name and number in bright gold.

Above my locker was a strip of white athletic tape with "Malcolmson–24" scribbled across it in black Sharpie marker. Maybe it wasn't quite as nice or permanent as the other lockers, but that was *my* name with *my* number above *my* locker in the USC locker room. I stood mesmerized, looking at that "24." I thought 24 was just the perfect number: *24 hours in a day, 24 karat gold, and of course, the legendary baseball player Willie Mays wore number 24.* It was such a balanced and cool-looking number. I was in a bit of a trance standing in front of that locker, listening to the showers running and feeling the damp steam accumulating in my musty little corner.

Shaken from my stupor, I realized that Tino had charged off again without me. I raced after him and finally caught up with him just as we reached the hallway, where he jabbed his thumb to the left and curtly said, "Go to the trainer."

I stood at the entrance to the training room, where a series of stations were set up to evaluate the walk-ons. Whisked away to the first station, I was barraged with health history questions regarding surgeries, allergies, medications, and past injuries as well as anything that might raise a red flag regarding being "fit" to compete. I was completely open and honest about everything.

Well, almost everything. Seven months earlier I had what I referred to as a "minor" incident with my right shoulder during a casual intramural football game when I was diving to intercept the ball. I may have neglected to mention that this "minor" incident ended with a 911 call as well as an ambulance trip to a local hospital. Surrounded by gunshot and stabbing victims whose more urgent injuries caused me to repeatedly lose my priority in line, I lay writhing in pain for five hours before being diagnosed with a dislocated shoulder. I glossed over the incident, referring to it as "no big deal" because I really did not think it was. I zipped through the last two stations, meeting Dr. James Tibone, the team doctor, and taking a baseline concussion test before leaving the basement with my duties complete.

It was nearly impossible for me to believe, stepping out of the doors I had entered only forty-five minutes before, that my life had been forever changed. Walking in, I had been nothing more than a bewildered college newspaper reporter. Walking out, I was a full-fledged member of the 2006 Trojan football team with the credentials to prove it, a bona-fide playbook in my hand, and my name scrawled on a piece of white athletic tape above my locker.

It was only about noon, but it felt like another lifetime since I bolted out of bed that morning. I was flustered and needed some time to process what had just happened. I aimlessly wandered around on the landing just outside Heritage Hall while relishing the first chaos-free moments I had experienced since 9:44 a.m. Standing at the top of those stairs, I was blinded by the brilliant California sun climbing in the cloudless, pale-blue sky. I stood cocooned in a pocket of silence while the campus bustled around me.

In an instant, on the wings of a gentle breeze, an extraordinary, undeniable sense pervaded my heart. It was as if God whispered into my ear, *I have a great purpose for you in this.* It wasn't actually a whisper or an audible voice at all, and it was barely distinguishable at first. In fact, had I not paused to listen, I may have missed it altogether. It wasn't something manufactured by me. In fact, there was no me in this at all. That thought was almost laughable. It was so much bigger than me, an absolutely, positively, unmistakably rock-solid message I could not deny and would never forget. The initial thrill of making the team paled in comparison to the profound realization that this wasn't about me at all.

I have a great purpose for you in this.

Just as movie credits scroll up a dark screen, a series of thoughts scuttled through my mind: *wasn't trying to make the team . . . newspaper reporter . . . super skinny . . . haven't played football since fifth grade . . . about to graduate . . . shouldn't be here.*

This wasn't simply phenomenal. It was impossible.

In my mind's eye, I dropped to my knees in awe, knowing I was on holy ground. That scenario probably only lasted about five seconds, but those five seconds would be cemented in my memory. In the months to come, I would need to draw on the strength and conviction of those five seconds repeatedly in order to survive.

I glanced over to make sure that the sheet with my name was, in fact, still taped to the door. And the craziness of the morning just seemed to slip away—this was real. About an hour before, everything was happening at warp speed, and now I floated down the concrete steps. I was quite relieved to find my unlocked bike still resting haphazardly in the bike rack, which meant I had actually experienced two miracles in one day.

It is difficult to describe the euphoria I felt as I pedaled lazily along, just one hand on the handlebars, my face drenched in sunlight, soaking in every single minute of this experience. It took me at least twice as long to get home as I dawdled, the adrenaline rush slowly dwindling away. I'm sure I was quite a sight, still wearing the clothes I had slept in the night before, a silly grin plastered on my face.

After parking my bike and quietly slipping up to my room, I immediately collapsed on the floor in a heap and silently prayed that no one would disturb me. I rolled over on my back, pressed my hands over my eyes, and welcomed the peace and quiet to sort out my thoughts.

My brief respite was interrupted by my friend David standing in the doorway. "Are you okay, Ben?"

"I know this sounds crazy, but I just made the football team," I said. In a matter of minutes, there was a steady stream of stunned well-wishers and curiosity seekers parading through my room while my phone rang incessantly.

The news spread like wildfire and elicited various reactions from my friends, from questioning and disbelief to excitement and elation. Since I was truly at a loss for words to explain it all, I simply kept offering up that sacred playbook as irrefutable evidence that I was telling the truth.

After two hours of nonstop visitors and commotion, I knew it was time for me to get my head back in the game—the actual game I was supposed to be covering at the Pac-10 Basketball Tournament at the Staples Center downtown. Unable to contain my excitement, I made a call to Gary Klein on my way to the game. I didn't know how to ease into the news, so I cut right to the chase and blurted out, "Hey, Gary, it's Ben. You won't believe this, but I tried out for the football team to write an article, and I made the team." Completely taken aback, he burst into an incredulous laugh, and I found myself chuckling right along with him. Once he had a chance to catch his breath, he congratulated me, saying, "That is so cool, Ben. I can't wait to write an article about you."

The last game of the night, between Washington and Oregon, started at 8:30 p.m., and I decided to head home at halftime as the excitement of the day finally caught up with me. Driving down Figueroa Street, I began to return some of the forty-plus calls that had blown up my phone over the past eight hours.

One of my first calls was to my dad, and since he knew nothing about my story idea or the tryouts, the whole thing sounded ludicrous to him. He was very pragmatic and extremely skeptical. "What about graduation and getting a job? How will your body be able to hold up? Why in the world would they want you on that team?" After all, the last time he had seen me in a football uniform was eleven years ago, when I was sitting in the front seat of our Honda station wagon begging him to let me quit playing. He was convinced there was something else going on and said emphatically, "You better check the calendar and make sure it isn't April Fools' Day. This has to be a joke the football team is pulling on you."

He concluded our conversation on an even more discouraging note. "You have never played football before, and you are going to get hurt." He was right about that. His callous response, which honestly voiced my own doubts and fears, hurt me before I had even taken a hit on the field.

After parking my car in the alley behind the fraternity house, I

dragged myself up the stairs and toppled into bed. Being an introvert, I was completely drained by all that social interaction, and as
my head hit the pillow at about eleven o'clock, the magnitude of it all
came crashing down. I instantly fell into a deep sleep. Awakening
several times during the night, I fought to convince myself that it
wasn't a dream. As I relived the series of events again and again, each
time I reached the same conclusion: *Whoa, this is for real. I am a
member of the 2006 Trojan football team.*

Spring break began the next day, and Colorado was the perfect
vacation for me, a wonderfully therapeutic time to reflect on the crazy
week I had just experienced and to look forward to what I fantasized
about as being the best days of my life. While my fraternity brothers
went out skiing, I didn't want to risk falling and reinjuring my shoulder, although I hadn't had any trouble with it since my incident. Instead, I stayed in the condo to write and rewrite my final *Daily Trojan*
articles until they were perfect. Since they would be my last stories, I
became wildly sentimental and obsessed with excellence.

While working on my articles was exhilarating, my other project that week was sobering and scared me to death. The first time I
cracked the cover of my playbook, my heart nearly stopped. Flipping
through those pages was like reading hieroglyphics, and without any
understanding of football terminology, I was completely lost. This
playbook simply didn't compare to the playbook on *Madden*.

Being a good student, I had developed excellent study skills, and
when I was facing a difficult subject in the past, repeatedly exposing
myself to the material had proven successful. Using that approach, I
opened the playbook again and again, hoping each time it would
make more sense than the time before. But honestly, I began to think
I could look at this information every day for the next forty years

with the same result: complete bewilderment. And as mind blowing as the last week had been, I was forced to face my greatest fear of all. *What if I can't cut it on the team?*

Up to this point, the physicality of the game and whether my body could hold up had been my biggest concerns. I really hadn't given much thought to the intellectual component of football. Completely naive, I had never considered how complicated the game actually is. Frustration mounted every time I opened that book. I was rapidly overwhelmed and began to entertain serious doubts about how I was going to figure this out, since I knew I couldn't ask Kiffin for help and didn't really know anyone who had played college football.

As I traveled to Colorado, my mind had been filled with big dreams and delightful possibilities of donning the famed USC jersey and running out of the Coliseum tunnel, but on the trip back to LA, I faced the harsh reality of what lay before me. With plenty of time to think, I began to grasp the severity of the predicament in which I found myself. I did not care for contact sports and had an aversion to being hit. On top of that, I had made virtually no headway in deciphering the playbook and had no viable plan for exactly how to tackle that.

The indisputable fact was that I did not belong on this team. After watching practice for three years, it's not like I didn't know what I was walking into. These guys were monstrous, and I had heard firsthand the deafening *thud*s and seen the vicious hits they inflicted on one another. They were bigger than I was, stronger than I was, and possessed infinitely more knowledge about how to play the game. *Who am I kidding?*

Looking back, it might have been prudent to listen to my head instead of my heart. As the reality of what I was about to do continued to sink in, I was absolutely terrified. But my lifelong fear of failure—coupled with my dad's "you're not a quitter" admonishment when I was a kid—were much more powerful than my fear of the future, and I never once entertained the thought of backing out.

WALK ON
Hearing God's Whisper

When you pause long enough to listen and shut out the noisy world, you will hear God's gentle whisper, a whisper guaranteed to carry you through whatever you're facing. What you hear might be similar to what I heard on the steps—*I have a great purpose for you in this*—or it could be something unique and wondrous just for you. Will you tune out the noise and stop to listen for the whisper of God in your life?

> As Elijah stood there, the LORD passed by, and a mighty windstorm hit the mountain. It was such a terrible blast that the rocks were torn loose, but the LORD was not in the wind. After the wind there was an earthquake, but the LORD was not in the earthquake. And after the earthquake there was a fire, but the LORD was not in the fire. And after the fire there was the sound of a gentle whisper.
>
> —1 Kings 19:11–12

10

Eighteen Hours

I submitted my final articles to the *Daily Trojan* on Sunday, March 19. As I pressed the Send button, I felt like I was standing in the eye of a hurricane where the winds were calm, but I knew the storm was coming. In fact, it was headed right for me with its gale-force winds being driven by all my anxious thoughts: getting hit, learning the playbook, getting hit, the first team meeting, getting hit, earning the respect of the coaches, getting hit, making friends on the team, and getting hit.

I had begun a somewhat gruesome countdown to the fateful moment when I would take that first hit, and right then it was just beginning . . . *forty-eight hours until I get hit.* Over the course of the next couple of days, I would continue that countdown nearly every hour, imagining who would inflict that first hit, what it would feel like, and if I would live to tell about it.

My first thought on Monday morning was, *Thirty-one hours until I get hit!* I attended my classes, completely distracted, watching the clock and thinking about the first team meeting that was scheduled for 5:30 p.m. I arrived at Heritage Hall at 5:15, did a quick scan when I entered the auditorium, and located a couple of the other walk-ons sitting near the front in the third row on the right, so I slipped into the aisle seat next to them. I was very pleased to see no demarcation line of "us" (the walk-ons) and "them" (the guys who were officially on the roster). It appeared we were all going to be treated the same, and I prayed I would not hear the words "newspaper guy" over the next ninety minutes.

This particular Trojans team had a whopping fifty-four players who would eventually play in the NFL, more than enough to fill an entire NFL roster. Even the caliber of the walk-ons already playing on the team was extremely high, and one blond beast in particular would garner a tremendous amount of respect and be awarded a scholarship in the fall. Good ol' Clay Matthews was awkward and a bit insecure at that point in his career, but he would rapidly come into his own and be named co–Special Teams Player of the Year twice at USC before being selected in the first round of the 2009 NFL draft by the Green Bay Packers, where he eventually earned All-Pro linebacker honors.

This was the same room where I had attended the informational walk-on meeting. I was looking forward to seeing Coach Carroll in action again and anxious to discover more of what he was like behind the scenes. He had come a long way since he stood at the podium in front of Heritage Hall on his first day in December 2000 and summed up his vision for the future in ten very powerful words: "Do things better than they have ever been done before."

At this point, his program was most certainly living out that vision. He was arguably the best college coach in the country, and his reputation for developing winners was at an all-time high. Carroll is one of only five coaches in college football history to have seven straight seasons with two or fewer losses, and in his nine seasons at

USC, he produced twenty-seven first-team All-Americans, fifty-six NFL draft picks, and three Heisman Trophy winners.

When the meeting started at exactly 5:30 p.m., Coach Carroll exploded with energy and enthusiasm while pacing back and forth in the front of the auditorium. Dressed in his trademark khaki pants, white long-sleeved USC T-shirt, and white "old man" athletic shoes, he welcomed everyone to spring football with, "I am so fired up to be here and to have all of us back together!" His blue eyes flashed like lightning.

I had always admired the way Coach Carroll handled the press and navigated their questions with his communication skills. But now, watching him in this team meeting, I saw him truly in his element. This was, without a doubt, what he was born to do. Within the first thirty seconds, the tryouts and my articles faded away, almost as if they had never happened. It would have been very easy to forget I had been a reporter. So caught up in the team spirit and the enthusiasm of the rest of the guys, I thought, *Here we go. This is real.*

His mantra, "It's all about the ball," would be repeatedly drilled into our heads at every meeting, every practice, every game, and every waking hour we were a part of Trojan football. He also stressed the importance of "the three rules," while cradling a football in his hand, which was poised above his head as if he were a shot-putter.

"Rule number one," he began, "is *Protect the team,* which means we take care of each other and are always thinking of what's best for our teammates. We are a family, these are your brothers, and you don't allow *anything* to break you up." He paused to make sure everyone was paying attention before continuing. "Rule number two," he said, "*No whining, no complaining, no excuses* is pretty straight-forward. You are only to engage in positive self-talk, always creating and emphasizing the positive. And rule number three," he said, "is *Be early*. Being early is a sign of respect, both for yourself and the people around you."

Those three rules really resonated with me. Of course, I loved rule number one and the idea of being part of a new family where my brothers would be taking care of me. And rule number two had been easy for me to practice since I spent so much time alone during my childhood. *Be early* was all about self-discipline, which appealed to me as well. Of course, I still had to figure out the whole playbook/survival thing, but at least when it came to the three rules, I knew I was destined for success.

Coach Carroll talked about the style of football the Trojans were known for: great effort, great enthusiasm, great toughness, and playing smart. I looked around the room, and sitting within a few rows of me were the stars of USC football, including Dwayne Jarrett, Steve Smith, Rey Maualuga, Brian Cushing, and John David Booty. And every single one of those guys, along with the other eighty-plus in the room, was held in rapt attention. It was as if Coach Carroll's very lifeblood was being infused into our veins and we just could not absorb it fast enough.

"Competition is the central theme of our program," Carroll declared with the excitement of a zealous salesman. "We compete at *everything* around here. And if we're competing to be our best, nothing can stop us."

While every coach and every athlete talks about competition, for Coach Carroll it is a way of life. Competition is a central focus of everything he does. In his words, "You are either competing or you're not," and there is no room on his team for someone who isn't always "in relentless pursuit of a competitive edge."

Coach Carroll then dismissed us into two groups; the defense went downstairs to meet with defensive coordinator Nick Holt, while the offense stayed put and met with offensive coordinator Steve Sarkisian, otherwise known as Sark. Sark took up right where Coach Carroll left off. He was incredibly likable and very engaging, and his enthusiasm was infectious. He wasted no time with introductions, small talk, or philosophy but dove headfirst into highlighting the "explosive and exciting" offense, rapid-firing through various plays. I opened my playbook, desperately trying to follow along, but I was so lost. I hastily slipped back into the comfort of reporter mode and scribbled furiously with hopes of sorting it out later.

One of Sark's key points was that we were going to be better this year. Which would sound like what you would expect to hear from just about any coach, but for a team that had just won thirty-four straight games and two national championships and boasted two Heisman Trophy winners on the same team, that sounded like a tall order. Unfortunately, in this case, the old adage that you are only as good as your last game struck a very painful chord with the Trojans. That's because the infamous Rose Bowl game against Texas less than three months earlier would have been their thirty-fifth straight win and their third straight national championship, but it ended in the most devastating way possible, on a heartbreaking touchdown with just nineteen seconds to go. The plan for "being better" this year was outlined by Sark's "Guidelines for the 2006 Trojan Offense."

Several guidelines caught my attention. One was *Be physical,* since I was sure that would involve contact and pain, two things I was guaranteed to experience in the coming months. Another potentially problematic one was *Play fast—you play fast by knowing what to do,* considering it was becoming increasingly clear to me that I had absolutely no idea what I was doing. My enthusiasm about the ability to master the three rules was being rapidly overshadowed by the complex details of the whole football thing. It would have been easy to succumb to doubt and fear, but I needed only to return to the moment on the steps when I heard that divine whisper—*I have a great purpose for you in this*—to keep my hopes alive.

We were immediately shuffled to the next meeting, which was broken down by position, and I found myself smack dab in the middle of the eight wide receivers and Coach Kiffin. We were really like a small brotherhood, five scholarship athletes and three walk-ons, and the mood was much looser here with a lot of joking around. While I had been lucky so far, Steve Smith decided to start razzing me about being "the newspaper guy," and the rest of the guys jumped in to tease me as well. I was relieved when the focus shifted to the next guy up.

Kiff laid out his expectations loud and clear; there was to be no walking on the field. We were expected to run to every drill. He went on to emphasize, "You will not be babied; do not be sensitive. I'm not here to be your friend." He paused for a minute, letting that soak in and then added, "Why am I here? To take you where you cannot take yourself." *Compassion* was not a part of his dictionary, and being injured was no excuse for missing practice.

Once the meeting was dismissed, I took a moment to introduce myself to the other wide receivers and tried to be friendly. Before I left, Kiff called me over and introduced me to a sharp, all-American, athletic-looking guy in his early twenties named Yogi Roth, who was a graduate assistant helping with the wide receivers. After walking on as a wide receiver and earning a scholarship at the University of Pittsburgh, he went to USC to serve under Coach Carroll's tutelage.

Kiff's words were direct and to the point: "Yogi, you are in charge of Ben. Teach him everything he needs to know, and, Ben, if you have any questions, talk to Yogi."

While he didn't say it directly, the implication was clear: "Don't talk to me." Although this handoff was obviously not a compliment, I was too naive to understand that he was pawning me off on Yogi. My thinking was, *Sweet, I am getting a great resource, and I am going to take full advantage and learn everything I can from Yogi.*

I rode my bike back to the fraternity house, and phrases from the meeting kept echoing in my mind like metal cleats in a concrete tunnel: "relentless pursuit of a competitive edge," "not going to be babied," "we are going to be better," "play fast," "be physical," and that nagging fear I could not escape.

Only eighteen hours until I am going to get hit.

No wonder I couldn't concentrate on anything for the rest of the night, and the last note I wrote on my yellow legal pad was "Therapeutic to write all this stuff because it was so overwhelming."

The really pathetic thing was that I had no idea how good I had it that day. The worst was yet to come.

WALK ON
Finding Peace

When the elation of making the team collided with my fear of getting hit along with the complexities of the playbook, I felt anxious and overwhelmed. I imagine you have been there too. In fact, you might be facing a situation like that right now. Whether it's the challenge of a new opportunity or the hassles of a nagging struggle, we all wrestle with stress, worry, and restlessness in our lives. How would your life be different if you could be free of worry and filled with peace?

> Don't worry about anything; instead, pray
> about everything. Tell God what you need,
> and thank him for all he has done. Then you
> will experience God's peace, which exceeds
> anything we can understand. His peace will
> guard your hearts and minds as you live in
> Christ Jesus.
>
> **—Philippians 4:6–7**

Boom!

It is certainly not unusual for a college student to wake up in a strange place with no recollection of how he got there. But when I found myself standing on the sideline in the middle of practice, instead of running plays on the field where I belonged, I was baffled. Taking a quick inventory, I discovered that all my limbs were still attached, so whatever happened must not have been that serious. But man, my head hurt.

I tried to focus on the field, but instead of the standard eleven guys on each side of the ball, it looked like each player now had a double and they were all moving in extremely slow motion. And for some reason, although it was a sunny day, a thick blanket of fog had mysteriously settled over the practice field. Light seemed to intensify the throbbing in my head, so I closed my eyes, hoping that the muddled feeling would go away. It was as if my brain cells had been hopelessly scattered and were desperately trying to find their way home.

This wasn't the first time I had taken a hard hit, since we were already two weeks into practice. A few days earlier I had been running a kickoff coverage drill where my assignment was to sprint down the field and get around six-foot, 250-pound Oscar Lua and six-two, 230-pound Brad Walker on my way to tackling the ball carrier. At 165 pounds, I was outweighed by over 300 pounds. Picture a Chihuahua taking on a Doberman pinscher.

No, make that two Doberman pinschers.

I knew we were going to run the drill multiple times, and although I was fairly sure it probably wasn't going to end well, I ran down the field as fast as I could each time and prayed for a different outcome.

I felt like Charlie Brown, who ran up to kick the football thinking that *this* time, Lucy might actually leave it in place. But every time, he landed flat on his back. After six trips down the field, where I ended up exactly like Charlie Brown each time, on trip number seven, Lua and Walker smirked at me while offering this advice: "Next time slow down before you get here, and we'll take it easy on you."

My notebook entry from that day read, "I'm still lost and getting yelled at a lot now."

Not only was my body being battered at practice; my introduction to the weight room brought a whole new kind of pain. Since in fifth grade we were too young to pump iron, I had never really set foot in a weight room before, unless I count the handful of times I walked through the weight room to get to track practice in high school.

I stood wide eyed and gawked at row upon row of gleaming silver weight machines. There were dozens of different machines with racks and weights and pulleys as well as dumbbells and barbells and kettlebells and a bunch of equipment I could not identify. *And I thought the playbook was confusing! How in the world am I going to find my way through this maze of metal?*

Of course, for the others guys on the team, this was like a home away from home, and they knew exactly what to do since they had all been lifting weights for years. I was particularly apprehensive about anything that would put stress on my weak shoulder and did my best to protect it during bench presses and similar exercises. This room, I was convinced, was actually a cleverly disguised torture chamber. My notebook entry that day consisted of just one word in all caps: KILLER.

The opening day of practice had been special when I pulled that number 24 jersey over my head for the first time. Filled with a healthy mix of giddiness and fear, I made my trek down the hallway to the field. Even the *clickety-clack* cadence of my rubber cleats on the concrete floor seemed to tap out a tune full of anticipation.

The hallway known as the All-American Walk was steeped in history. The cardinal-colored walls were plastered with large color photos of the dozens of All-American Trojan football players in action, and I could almost feel the spirit of those guys offering me an unspoken welcome. The double doors were propped open to a glorious, sunny, beautiful Southern California day, and I inhaled the warm spring air while heading toward the practice field.

As a reporter carrying my notebook, I had walked through Goux's Gate, named in honor of USC coaching icon Marv Goux, for three years. I had come to feel that this was where I belonged. I thrived as a student journalist and felt at home in that role. But now, as I walked through that same gate as a football player carrying his helmet, things had definitely changed.

The air pulsed with ear-splitting music punctuated by a booming bass, and there were people milling around everywhere. Hundreds of passionate fans attended practices, which were always open to the public, and they stood behind a string of multicolored pennants flapping in the breeze. Many held footballs and Sharpies in hopes of snagging an autograph from their favorite player.

My teammates were scattered haphazardly around the field, stretching, tossing a football, or going through other first-day-of-practice rituals. The freshly chalked white lines were so perfect and so precise that I couldn't imagine stepping on them and messing them up. The reporters and camera operators mingled among the fans, pens poised, hoping to discover the perfect angle for their season-opening story. All in all, the atmosphere felt much more like that of a rock concert than a football practice, and my combination of giddiness and fear became short on giddy and big on fear.

I had grown so comfortable being a member of the press corps and would have loved to hang out with Gary Klein and the rest of the crew for some encouragement. But before practice Coach Carroll had informed me that he had instituted a gag order, which meant I would not be available for any interviews either before or after practice. He and the PR department thought that having a walk-on as the center of attention might be a distraction, and since I just wanted to blend in and be one of the guys, the gag order was fine by me.

Two sharp air-horn blasts signaled the beginning of practice, and like a group of marine recruits, everyone hustled over and lined up on those pristine white lines in groups of eight, stretching the width of the field. I had absolutely no idea where I was supposed to go, so like a puppy on the heels of his master, I followed the other wide receivers, mimicking their every move.

On Coach Carlisle's whistle, the first man in each line broke into a 40-yard sprint; the others quickly followed at two-second intervals. Over the course of the next two hours, as challenging as it was for me to keep up physically, the mental gymnastics were much more difficult. I struggled to make sense of continuously chirped words and phrases that I was completely unfamiliar with: *Hang your hams, sprinter's stance, quad stretch, Saigon squat, post, slant, dig, out, corner.* During the stretching, I was able to fake it by copying the movements of the other players, and once we split into the individual drills, I employed my successful tryout tactic: I stood at the back of the line until I figured it out.

And between the commotion on the field and the warning bells of doubt ringing in my head, I strained to hear that precious whisper: *I have a great purpose for you in this.*

Throughout practice, chaos ensued, courtesy of Coach Carroll. Not only did he allow it; he encouraged it. While most coaches insisted upon closed practices and operated behind a cloak of secrecy to protect their coaching methods and plays from the prying eyes of their opponents, Coach Carroll believed the more distraction for his players, the better. It wasn't unusual to see celebrities such as Snoop Dogg stepping in as a guest coach or Will Ferrell stirring things up with his crazy antics, including showing up at practice dressed as the Carroll-created superhero Captain Compete.

And the revelation that Carroll actually hoped for the worst possible weather conditions came as a complete surprise to me. I remember the first rainy-day practice, when I learned just how difficult it was to catch a wet football. It repeatedly slipped from my hands as if it had been smeared with grease. At the end of that day, with my shorts plastered to my legs, my gray T-shirt soaked through and clinging to my torso, and water trickling down my legs into my soggy socks before puddling in my cleats, I thanked God I didn't live in Seattle.

So whether Coach Carroll manufactured the distractions or got some help from Mother Nature, he made sure we were never without them. He firmly believed that if our team could practice well amidst blaring music, celebrity sightings, adverse weather, and anything else he could throw at us, we would be adequately prepared for the LA Coliseum overflowing with ninety thousand frenzied fans or the hostile stadium of an opponent. In fact, it was his hope that game day would seem calm and controlled compared to our daily practices.

In addition to adjusting to the play on the field and learning how to work out in the weight room, I found that understanding the equipment was much more complicated than I had imagined. Putting my shoulder pads on for the first time was a somewhat embarrassing experience. Shoulder pads may look simple, but they consist of an intricate series of straps, buckles, and laces, making them a distant cousin of the straitjacket.

I had really been looking forward to the day I would suit up with my shoulder pads and my skinny little frame would transform into the hulking broad-shouldered look most of the guys came by naturally. After all, shoulder pads are the one piece of equipment that makes a football player *look* like a football player. I proudly lifted those cardinal and white shoulder pads off the hook in my locker, pulled them over my head, and locked the elastic straps in place.

I then tried to stretch my jersey over the pads while pulling and tugging and wrestling my arms through the holes. All the while I was thinking that I had to be some kind of contortionist to do it. Then it dawned on me: *This isn't going to happen.* I was going to need to reverse my course and get the jersey back over my head before someone noticed what a rookie I was. I saw a teammate a few lockers away who had put his jersey on the pads *before* he pulled the whole thing over his head. So I uncinched, unbuckled, and lifted the pads back over my head as quickly as possible, hoping that no one was paying attention.

Of course, the more I rushed, the more discombobulated things became. Panic was setting in because practice was about to start, and I knew I couldn't be late. I dropped to my hands and knees and pinned the shoulder pads between my legs and the floor while attempting to pull and stretch and twist the jersey over the pads. The plastic was slippery, the jersey was slick, and I could not get a handle on either one.

It was comedic, really; the minute I would get one side over the pads and go to work on the other side, the first one would pop off, and I would be back to square one. I swear, it felt like I was wrestling a slimy alligator. I finally got the jersey on the pads and slipped the entire unit over my head. Practice hadn't even started yet, and I was already sweating and exhausted.

In that dazed moment on the sideline, I knew my wrestling match with the shoulder pads was several days earlier, but I wasn't sure exactly how many days ago. While I didn't know it at the time, I would later learn that the play where I got my first concussion with no memory of how I got there was actually the second of two facemask-to-facemask meetings that afternoon with Rey Maualuga, the six-foot-two, 260-pound eventual second-round draft pick of the Cincinnati Bengals.

The first time I, um, "bumped" into Rey, I had just sprinted down the field, feeling fearless and invincible, executed a near perfect pivot, loaded up in a knees-bent, arms-taut, solid blocking position (especially for someone who hadn't really ever blocked before), and braced for impact before unceremoniously being slammed to the ground, landing spread eagle with my face mask planted firmly in the turf. I didn't know what had happened or why I was face down on the field, but it didn't take long for unbidden memories of my youth football days to come flooding back.

I imagine that encounter looked a bit like one of those ginor-mous monster trucks running over a poor little Volkswagen. I re-member thinking, *I've gotta get up; I've gotta get up,* but I was so disoriented that I had no idea which direction "up" actually was. I could hear the coach repeatedly yelling, "We're going back; we're running it again." I didn't have time or the presence of mind to con-sider that perhaps it would not be wise to try that again. I mean, I was still alive, so why tempt fate two times in row?

Before I knew it, I was back on the line and ready to run the play again. I started on my assignment just the way I did before, running full speed down the field, but this time I was panting and out of breath, partly due to the exertion but mostly due to the sheer terror of facing that guy one more time. Like a racehorse breaking from the starting gate, he came thundering toward me, and this time he smelled fear. He locked eyes with me, a vicious grin playing on the corners of his mouth, clearly ecstatic that he would get to flatten me once more. He lowered his helmet and rammed into me like a torpedo—and that was the last thing I remembered.

The following day we had a film review session led by defensive line coach Dave Watson. A typical old-school football coach, he be-lieved the best way to motivate his players was through intimidation and domination. Nicknamed Sweaty, he was easy to spot as he ran around the field barking orders and dishing out insults while leaving a trail of sweat drippings wherever he went. He was the bane of my existence during those spring practices as he conjured up painful memories of my brutal youth football coach.

A film review session was part affirmation and part humiliation. The coaches highlighted the things in practice or a game that went well and pointed out specific areas needing improvement. The video was projected onto a gigantic screen, making the plays really come to life. We were all seated in those cushy theater seats in the auditorium, and Sweaty was manning the clicker that allowed him to fast-forward, rewind, or pause if he wanted to break down a specific play or call out an individual player's performance. I remembered one of Coach Kiffin's admonitions, "The film is your résumé," and understood that my performance on film would be the way my teammates would view me.

There were more than a hundred plays at practice each day, so even though I knew my shellacking had probably been captured on film, since I really couldn't remember exactly what happened, I was hoping it might slip by unnoticed. I mean, there are twenty-one other guys on the field at a time, so I had good odds, right?

I was intently watching the screen on every play, prepared to judge my performance and see if I looked the part of a football player. As the film rolled on, I was able to identify myself on several plays and thought, *Okay, that's not so bad. I look like somewhat of an athlete.* And then *the play* appeared on the screen and disappeared without Sweaty even making a mention of it. As he moved on to critique the next play, I was thinking, *Whew, I dodged that bullet.* Then I heard one of the guys holler out, "Whoa, whoa, whoa, back it up." I slunk down in my seat, dreading what was to come. The next time through *the play,* a smattering of giggles erupted, and then the players chided him to rewind it again.

The third time through, the room erupted in uncontrollable laughter, and I cringed while sliding even lower, just inches from slipping off the seat completely, and wishing I could disappear. By the fourth time, the guffaws came fast and furious, and guys were nearly doubled over.

With each subsequent replay, the room went silent for a split second in anticipation, and then whispers of "Wait for it, wait for it" began to build until the instant Rey made the hit, when a chorus of "Boom!" exclamations reverberated through the room as my scrawny little body was launched into the air like a teddy bear's before landing lifeless on the field. On the outside I tried to laugh it off, but the humiliation on the inside was even more agonizing than the physical pain.

In spite of *the play* and my splitting headache, I was cautiously optimistic about my progress over the past several weeks. The morning after our first practice, I was as sore as I had been following the tryouts and struggled to get out of bed. And since then I had been battered and beat up and had spent an awful lot of time dragging myself off the turf. The stress on a football player's body has been well documented and likened to the impact of an automobile accident. I would imagine the stress on a non-football-player's body would be much more like a train wreck. My Costco-sized bottle of Advil helped numb the pain, and I tried to focus on the gradual improvement I was seeing.

My three weightlifting workouts a week, along with my personalized nutrition plan that emphasized shoveling in the calories, were making me stronger and building muscle mass on my scrawny, scarecrow frame. I understood the difference between a bench press and a military press, and my weight-lifting power cleans were getting better every day. I hadn't experienced any pain with my shoulder, and it was feeling really solid.

I had gone from a clueless rookie who couldn't even put on his pads to getting dressed in record time. That youth football player who hid on the sidelines was a very distant memory, and as my confidence began to build, I wanted to get more reps in practice every day. I became distracted during classes since I much preferred studying the playbook to studying my textbooks. I scribbled notes and diagrams and questions for Yogi on my yellow pad while I sat in class and mused, *Football is always on my mind, but I don't have a football mind yet. That's all I'm thinking about in class, but it's not quite clicking for me.*

Along with my body and my mind, my goals were also undergoing a dramatic transformation. Initially, the fear of being hit and the complexity of the playbook focused me on one simple goal: surviving to see my twenty-first birthday. But now as my physical strength along with my understanding of the playbook steadily increased, my goals were becoming significantly more ambitious, and I dared to dream about playing in a real game. I knew it was still a long shot, but my work ethic and overachiever mind-set nurtured that dream.

Although I had come a long way, my football prowess was still wildly underwhelming, so I wasn't really included as one of the guys. But there were a few of my teammates who were very welcoming, especially our placekicker, Mario Danelo. He was extremely talented and possessed strong NFL potential, having just broken the NCAA single-season records with eighty-three extra points and eighty-six attempts the previous season. While some of the guys of his caliber were a bit standoffish, Mario was down to earth, friendly, and engaging. He always wore a smile and seemed genuinely happy. Whenever someone asked him how he was doing, he would always reply that he was "livin' the dream." His uplifting personality was magnetic and infectious, and he was truly a joy to be around, either on the football field or in the locker room.

He quickly became one of my closest friends on the team, just as he was with most of his other teammates.

With each passing day, I was actually beginning to believe that I could make a run at playing this game. And the whisper from the top of the steps, *I have a great a purpose for you in this,* continually echoed in my mind, and I was so fired up to see what that purpose was.

WALK ON
Perseverance

How we respond to the storms of life often determines our trajectory. Those early days of practice were grueling. My body, my mind, and my pride took a fierce beating. It would have been very easy to quit, and I'm sure several of the coaches would have been happy if I had. When trials come in all their various shapes and sizes, you have a decision to make: endure or quit. Will you choose to persevere amidst your challenges?

> Blessed is the man who perseveres under
> trial, because when he has stood the test,
> he will receive the crown of life that God
> has promised to those who love Him.
>
> **—James 1:12, BSB**

12

Dislocated

On April 6, during the third week of practice, my assignment was simply to block cornerback Kevin Thomas for three seconds.

One Mississippi, two Mississippi, three Mississippi.

And I have wondered countless times since that picture-perfect spring day, what would have happened if I had been able to hold that block.

While it hadn't been an easy three weeks, I was feeling more and more confident about my future on the team each passing day. The other guys had been living this football life for years and took most of it for granted. Since it was all so new to me, I still got excited about even the littlest things, like diving for a great catch during warm-ups. I was learning how to hit and, more importantly, how to take a hit. I was beginning to look like a football player, feel like a football player, and have the mind of a football player. And since the dream of every football player is to play a snap during a game, I was beginning to wonder, *Why not me?*

That Thursday afternoon was a normal practice day, and I was assigned to the scout team kickoff coverage unit, which would be facing off against our starting kickoff return team. The scout team plays a valuable role in practice: to mimic the competition. It's not really a fair fight, considering the scout team is made up of the smallest players on the team. But the scout team has a bunch of guys who are trying to prove themselves, and they fight like crazy to make things as game-like as possible for the starters.

In this particular drill, my assignment was to sprint about fifty yards down the field to tackle the ball carrier. Unfortunately, a large obstacle otherwise known as a blocker appeared in my path and pounded me. In fact, several times I was being double-teamed by two beastly blockers who were trying to keep me from reaching the guy with the ball, giving me a painful double pounding.

Imagine running a fifty-yard dash, wearing twenty pounds of bulky gear, while looking through a four-by-six-inch window in your facemask, and crashing full speed into a solid brick wall, a scene Yogi later described as being "lit up." Since Yogi had become a big-brother figure, his words were oddly soothing, and it felt like I was becoming a part of the family when I was being teased for surviving such a hit. Plus, I secretly celebrated after enduring each hit, thinking that surely I was nearing the tipping point and might soon be promoted from my lowly status, having somewhat earned my place among the guys. Since there are no backups on the scout team, I worked my tail off running that drill four times in a row and was relieved that practice would soon be over.

The final eleven-on-eleven drills were the closest we came to simulating a live game situation in practice, and Coach Carroll always made sure they were extremely competitive. With the sun beginning to set and the cool spring air settling over the field, I was called to sub for a wide receiver on one of the last plays of practice that day.

The quarterback, Mark Sanchez, called the play in the huddle and led the universal hand clap and "break" chant; then everyone lined up to get set for the play. The defense had to know it was going to be a running play since there was no way Sanchez would ever throw the ball to me. I lined up as an X receiver to the right, directly across from cornerback Kevin Thomas. Nicknamed Keto, he was eventually a third-round draft pick by the Indianapolis Colts. At six-one, with quick feet, long arms, and loose hips, Keto was able to turn and run with the maneuverability of a Maserati.

I got down in my stance, looked right across the line into his eyes, and saw a glint of amusement. He was inches from my face, and we both knew what was up. Keto was going to toy with me a bit, toss me aside, and go after the running back, hoping to make a tackle. While I would be fighting for my life, he wouldn't even break a sweat. I heard Sanchez call out the presnap cadence and then "Ready, GO!" The play erupted with everyone scrambling toward his assignment.

I had one duty on that play—to block Keto and make sure he did not get to the running back. To the casual observer, this didn't look like a horrific mismatch, as we were roughly the same height and weight. But that is where the similarities ended. Keto had at least ten years of football experience on me as well as a knowledge and expertise of technique I would never have. But all I had to do was hold that block for three seconds, and I would live to fight another play. No problem.

When you block, the objective is to jam your hands up under the breastplate of the opponent's shoulder pads while he tries to shuck you off. I had my fingers wrapped under his pads, and Keto was wiggling and swatting at me while likewise attempting to grab my pads and throw me off, much like a bucking bronco tries to launch his rider from his back. And just as the eight seconds required to score on that bucking bronco have been described as the most dangerous eight seconds in sports, the next three seconds were the most dangerous in my short career.

As the tussle ensued, my right hand got stuck under the breastplate of his shoulder pads, and while I pulled and tugged frantically, I could not free it. He flicked me off as easily as he would a fly and took off in hot pursuit of the running back. My shoulder dislocated completely as the force of his motion ripped my arm from the socket.

The pain was immediate, and it felt like my right arm had been completely severed from my body. I staggered backward, as if shot by a gunslinger in an old western, and used my left hand to reach for where I thought my right arm should be, although I wasn't sure it was still attached. I crumpled to the ground, wishing that the gunslinger had put me out of my misery. I heard the *smack* of helmets and the *thud* of pads, along with the assorted grunts and groans you would expect as a half ton of testosterone tackled the running back, just a few yards away from where I lay, moaning and writhing in pain.

It was the same shoulder as my "minor dislocation" the year before, and I knew in an instant it was bad. Russ, the head trainer, came rushing onto the field, knelt next to me, and said, "What's wrong?" Between desperate moans and thrashing around on my back, I whimpered through clenched teeth, "My shoulder is out."

Since I was right on the line of scrimmage, I heard Coach Carroll yell, "Okay, move it up," and the players moved up fifteen yards to run the play again. I was practically invisible. They just stepped over me and got right back to work.

In the meantime, Russ was trying to alleviate some of my pain

by repositioning my shoulder while saying, "Just relax; just relax."
Relax? I was experiencing more pain than I ever would have imagined a human being could withstand. In the span of about thirty
seconds, he popped my shoulder back into place on the field, and the
roaring tidal wave of agony that had been crashing over me immediately stilled. My entire body went limp, and I sank into the turf with
an "Aaaaaaaaaah" of relief.

Considering that the last time it happened I had spent nearly five
hours in the emergency room, thirty seconds was nothing. But somehow, I knew this wasn't the same. It felt worse, much worse. There
was no way I could have endured a five-hour wait this time. If I had
needed to wait even five more minutes, I would have blacked out
completely from the pain.

Russ and a couple other trainers helped me to the sideline and
into the dreaded trainers' tent, and they began to remove my shoulder pads. The initial searing pain was gone, but in its place was a dull
ache that was wildly intensified by any movement at all. Getting the
pads off was quite an ordeal as the trainer had to get my good arm
out first and then gingerly pull the whole apparatus over my head
without jostling my injured arm.

I slumped over on the training table, in my gray T-shirt soaked
with sweat, and dropped my chin to my chest. I heard the hum of the
small white injury cart as it pulled up beside me. To every football
player, that cart is the universal sign of defeat. If your injury is severe
enough to warrant this type of transport, you probably won't be back
anytime soon. When players see this cart on the field, they drop to a
knee, and fans reverently rise to their feet and offer a quiet clap of
consolation as the injured player is driven off. Everyone knows what
this means—it's serious.

I cradled my injured arm and gently slid onto that black vinyl seat next to the student trainer while asking myself, *How did this happen? For three seconds I was blocking Keto. Ten seconds later I was thrown to the ground. Within thirty seconds I was surrounded by trainers. In sixty seconds my shoulder had been popped back into place. Before four minutes ticked off the clock, I was carted away in humiliation.*

In less than five minutes, my career as a walk-on appeared to be over.

After a short drive to the medical center for x-rays, I returned to the locker room to get cleaned up. Alone in the locker room, I finally let the tears come, uninhibited. Not merely in response to the pain, but more the reality of what I was losing—the astonishing opportunity of a lifetime—and just when it was all coming together. My disappointment was on par with the pain, more than I believed I could withstand. Slipping my feet into my Rainbows, I shuffled to the training room, a broken man in every sense of the word, where the trainers completely packed my shoulder with bags of ice, tightly secured with several layers from a giant roll of plastic wrap.

When Russ arrived, I hesitantly asked him the questions I feared to voice. "What does this mean? How long am I out for?" He repeatedly dodged my questions, as if he didn't want to be the bearer of bad news. "Come back tomorrow," he told me.

Since I couldn't ride my bike, I left it locked up at Heritage Hall and plodded back to the house with my arm in a sling and the ice packs drip, drip, dripping on the sidewalk. Head bowed, eyes downcast, I welcomed the haze of isolation and despair that insulated me from the rest of the world. I could not climb up onto my top bunk, so my roommate grabbed my skimpy mattress and dragged it to the floor where it landed with a *thud*. Someone brought me a large stuffed backrest with padded arms so I could prop myself up against the wall, and there I sat, six feet of sorrow and pain. I knew it was really bad news, and that was why they wouldn't tell me how long the injury would keep me sidelined. They were just prolonging the inevitable.

Throughout that long and restless night, I wrestled with God and questioned His plan. *Why are You doing this? What about my purpose?* Those hours dragged on endlessly while I strained to hear a whisper in the darkness. My only solace came from a verse posted above our doorframe. I welcomed the words from 2 Corinthians 12:9 as they permeated my troubled soul: "My grace is sufficient for you, for my power is made perfect in weakness" (NIV).

When the sun came up the next morning, I had no energy or ambition to get out of bed. I forced myself to trudge back to Heritage Hall, looking exactly like I had twelve hours before—same clothes, same shoes, same sling, and same shroud of despondency surrounding me.

Chris Grosskopf was assigned as my trainer, and he was very kind and sympathetic as I sat on the training table once again with my legs dangling and my heart aching. He gently and tactfully began to prepare me for the truth by saying, "You are going to start rehabbing. You can't do anything today; it's too soon. But the sooner you start rehabbing, the quicker you will be back."

I dug into the last sentence about the speed of my recovery being linked to the start of my rehab and started pressing him: "Okay, when can I start? I need to get going." He obviously had consulted with Russ and gave me the same three-word response: "Come back tomorrow." He sent me to get an MRI before I left, but I walked away even more disheartened than when I walked in.

Unable to face reality, I went to the team meetings and practice as I had every day for the past three weeks, but instead of being an active participant, I stood on the sideline wallowing in my pity. It might seem strange that this was all so devastating to me. Anyone can understand the discouragement that accompanies a serious injury, but my reaction went way deeper than that. The fact was, I was only a walk-on with virtually no football background and very little skill who likely would never set foot on the field during a game. So why even try to come back? Just as Coach Carroll had said on the day of the tryouts, "If you make it, you'll be treated like you're a part of the team." I had tasted what it felt like to be part of the team and had reconfigured all my plans and dreams for the future. I simply wasn't ready to give it all up.

My pain intensified when I had to face Yogi—my coach, my mentor, my big brother, and the lone assistant who had taken an interest in me. His voice dripped with disappointment when he said, "Why didn't you tell me about that previous shoulder injury? You were hiding that from me, huh?" Hearing Yogi call me out for deceiving him crushed me. I was just barely on life support as it was, and that nearly pushed me into a flat line. I mumbled an apologetic response. "I wanted to play, and I didn't think it was that big of a deal. I never thought I would hurt it again."

The Trojan Huddle, the scrimmage that marked the end of spring practice, was scheduled for just a few days later, on Sunday, April 9. There were fifteen thousand enthusiastic fans in the Coliseum, all eager to get a glimpse of their beloved Trojans for the upcoming season. My parents, my grandparents, and my brother were flying in for the day to watch my first game in a USC uniform. I was still living in fantasyland, since I hadn't gotten any definitive news from the trainers, and I was actually thinking on the bus ride to the Coliseum that I could talk them into letting me play—with my arm in a sling. Yeah, right.

I headed straight to the training room and spent ten minutes trying to convince Russ that I could play, which was so ridiculous because I couldn't even move my arm. I emphatically said, "I think I can do it. I think I can do it." My desperation was so acute, I was unable to think clearly, and I'm sure Russ thought the painkillers were making me irrational.

With my shoulder packed in ice, I made my way out to the field through the tunnel well after kickoff. Man, how I wished I had run through that tunnel wearing my uniform for the first time with my team. Instead, I walked alone, wearing my gray shorts and my jersey while dreading what was waiting for me on the other side.

It was a blistering hot April day, and the blazing Southern California sun burned my face and increased the discomfort of the sling, while sweat poured into my eyes and down my neck. I didn't dare look up in the stands on the off chance that I might actually see my family. I had casually mentioned my injury but neglected to admit the severity of it, and I hadn't told them I wasn't going to play. I couldn't bear to see the price of my deception etched on their faces.

Coach Carroll jokingly said to me in passing, "Why don't you just spit on it and play?" *I wish, dude.* After halftime Russ connected me with team surgeon Dr. Tibone, who didn't bother to sugarcoat his doomsayer message as he scanned my MRI. "You have a torn labrum and a torn rotator cuff. If you don't have surgery and keep playing football, there is a 100 percent chance you will dislocate your shoulder again. If you don't have surgery and stop playing football, there is a 90 percent chance you will dislocate your shoulder again. The choice is up to you."

At the conclusion of the game, I met my family on the field, and they peppered me with questions faster than I could answer them. My dad seemed upset that they had flown all the way out for the game and I hadn't told them I was seriously injured. I had no defense, really, aside from being completely delusional about the reality of the situation. We made plans to meet up later for dinner, although all I really wanted to do was suffer alone.

On Tuesday, I told Dr. Tibone I was ready to move ahead with the surgery. I called my parents to let them know about my plans, and my mom's response startled me. She said she would be in Florida at a golf school on the day of my surgery and asked, "Can you move the date?"

No, I can't move it. Don't you realize how traumatic this is for me? At twenty years old, I should have been accustomed to such a self-centered reply from my mother, whose own needs typically over-shadowed the needs of those around her because of her struggles with alcohol. But kids never truly outgrow their desire to be genu-inely taken care of by their parents, and this brief exchange with my mother stung deep in my soul.

My protective instincts kicked in and my hyperindependent na-ture flared up. "Um, no, I honestly don't think I need you here." My dad agreed to fly out, which allowed me to wrap up the phone call without any conflict.

On Friday, I had a pre-op consult with Dr. Tibone, which cul-minated with a gloomy prognosis: "You won't be able to get back on

the football field for nine months." Although I had finally acknowledged the reality of my injury, I hadn't yet embraced the ramifica-
tions of it. And in that moment, I realized how badly I wanted to be
a member of that team. God promised me a purpose on those steps,
and I couldn't believe it would go unfulfilled. *Nine months? That's
January 2007! The season will be over! This can't be happening!* My
time as a USC football player appeared to be ending just as star-
tlingly as it had begun a few weeks earlier.

Over the next few days, as I was so desperate for even a glimmer
of hope, my mind drifted back to a speech Coach Carroll had given
in one of the recent team meetings. He said, "Doctors aren't the ones
that heal you; you determine when you are going to come back. If
the doctor says you are going to be out for four weeks, you make it
your goal to come back in two. You don't let their time lines determine when you are going to be back." And somehow his words,
combined with the echo from that whisper of purpose, would not
allow me to give up.

I knew I was on that team for a reason and was intent on seeing
it through, just as I had with every other challenge in my life since
that ten-year-old boy had pleaded with his father to let him quit
youth football. Quitting was simply not an option.

The surgery itself lasted about fifty minutes and involved an-
choring two separate tears of the labrum back to the shoulder socket.
After the operation, my dad drove me back to the fraternity house,
settled me onto my mattress on the floor, loaded me up with pain
pills, Gatorade, and pretzels, and left me to drift in and out of fitful
sleep all night.

He stopped by on his way to the airport the next morning, and
we went in to meet briefly with Coach Carroll, who seemed sincerely

interested in my recovery. And in true Coach Carroll form, he wouldn't let me leave without a postsurgery pep talk. "Let's get you back. Start the rehab. Let's get you going. Don't wait." While his sentiment was heartfelt and sincere, it might have been merciful of him to cut me loose and not sprinkle a bit of water on my seed of hope.

Had he known his words would give roots to my hope that would later be difficult to untangle, he might've wished he had never said them.

WALK ON
Questioning God's Plan

When I faced a serious injury and utter heartbreak, I began to question the message from God I heard in the whisper on the steps. I couldn't see past the discouragement and disheartenment. I'll bet you have been there too. In what areas of your life have you felt disappointed and abandoned by God?

> Who are you, a mere human being, to argue with God? Should the thing that was created say to the one who created it, "Why have you made me like this?"
>
> —Romans 9:20

13

Humiliated

Three days later, I would have given anything to have Rey Maualuga knock me unconscious when I received a text from the director of football operations, Dennis Slutak, that rattled me: "Hey! Come on into the office and bring your playbook."

My first response was absolute defiance. Everyone knew what it meant to turn in your playbook. You were getting kicked off the team. But there was no way they were cutting me; there had to be some mistake! I just went through reconstructive shoulder surgery and was fully committed to my rehab program. And I most definitely heard Coach Carroll say, "Let's get you back." I was on this team for a purpose! How dare Slutak take it upon himself to make this move? *Who does he think he is?*

Just a few hours later, I found out exactly who he thought he was when I stood warily in front of him, playbook in hand. "We are going to have to cut you from the team. Thank you for everything you have done for us during spring practice. We wish you the best of luck." He was curt and matter of fact, and as I grudgingly handed him my playbook, I became painfully aware that all those other moments when I thought I was at my lowest point were nothing compared to this one.

For the next three months, USC was kind enough to provide me access to the world-class treatment facilities as I went through rehab for my shoulder as if I were still a player. But since I wasn't really a USC athlete any longer, I felt like I was standing right back in front of my locker with my name above it on a strip of white athletic tape. I didn't belong. And while I tried to mask my inner feelings of inadequacy, there was little I could do to hide my outward appearance. Since I had been forced to turn in all my team gear, I had to work out in my old black Nike shorts and haggard white T-shirt. It was humiliating and humbling. But I faithfully followed my daily rehab regimen, while that distant whisper of purpose inspired me to work hard in hopes of regaining a spot on the team.

From the minute Coach Carroll placed his belief in me by putting me on the team, he gave me an infusion of confidence I had never experienced before. He saw something special in me, and that made me feel valued and important. Those feelings were somewhat foreign to me, and I was dead set on proving that his confidence hadn't been misplaced. Between Coach's faith in me and the endless hours Yogi had invested, I felt like I owed them an all-out effort to do everything within my power to get back on the team. The reality was that Coach and Yogi probably could not have cared less whether I returned to the team. In some ways, it would have meant less work and hassle if I didn't. What I had no way of knowing at the time was that their impression of my character, as I battled through this adversity, would have a tremendous effect on my future with both of them.

Coach Carroll was a very busy guy, and I knew that with all he had on his mind, it would be easy for him to forget about me. I decided it was imperative that I create opportunities where I could lobby to get back on the team. But I also knew that with his somewhat unpredictable summer schedule, creating those opportunities would not be easy. I needed to establish a surefire point of contact, and after careful consideration, I found the perfect location.

Since I knew he had to walk through the football headquarters' reception area on the way to and from his office, I chose a cushy, chocolate-brown leather couch as my lookout post for Operation Intercept Coach Carroll. A few days after my surgery, I launched my mission by approaching Coach's assistant, Christie, and asking if I could speak with him. She disappeared for a minute, then came back and said apologetically, "He's busy right now. Can you come back another time?" The next day, I returned with the same question and received the same answer, to which I steadfastly responded, "If he's busy, I can wait." Then I settled in on that couch. And wait I did, that day for one hour, and on subsequent days, I would sit there for two hours or more.

It was actually starting to irritate me. *Wow, the day I made the team, they stopped everything and ushered me into his office immediately. Now I can't even get a simple "How's it going, Ben?" out of the guy.*

I had scoped out the landscape of the couch so thoroughly that I knew exactly where I needed to sit to be out of Christie's line of sight because it was really awkward when our eyes met. But if I had been sitting there for a long while and she seemed absorbed in her work, I loudly repositioned myself, often accompanied by a brief cough, just to remind her that I was still there.

Since it was summer and I had just finished my undergrad degree, I wasn't really that busy. I had rehab early every morning and a valet job and grad school classes in the evenings, but I could devote almost every midday and afternoon to Operation Intercept Coach

Carroll. I'm sure some of the people in the office pitied the forlorn ex-player who sat resolutely on that couch for hours at a time, hoping for a second chance.

And some were probably irritated at my persistence, but that whisper had become a shout of conviction. I had a purpose on this team, and I wasn't going to give up until I found it. Finally, after watching me sit on that couch for several days, Christie felt sorry for me and found a way for me to get a minute with Coach Carroll so I could plead my case. "What can I do to get back on this team? Whatever I can do, I want to be on this team."

He paused for a moment, considered his words carefully, and said, "Just keep rehabbing and we'll see where we're at when you're done, and maybe we will put you back on the team." Now, I don't know whether he actually meant that or just said it to get me off his couch. But either way, I took it to mean that if my rehab went well, I would be back on the team.

Over the next several weeks, I continued my regular stakeouts on the couch, hoping to catch his eye so I could provide updates for him on my progress, like "Still rehabbing, Coach" or "Feeling better, Coach" or "I lifted five pounds today, Coach." Some days I didn't see him at all, and on the days I got a glimpse of him, I was lucky if he acknowledged me with a nod of his head or a wave of his hand or maybe a "Cool, keep it up" as he breezed past, hoping to get rid of me as soon as possible.

As the days wore on, that shout of conviction was in danger of being drowned out by a host of other voices. My dad was telling me it was time to get a job, and I started to wonder if I should pursue a backup plan in case the football thing didn't work out. When I was having a bad week of rehab or my shoulder was throbbing in the middle of the night or I was sprinting around some fancy mansion in Beverly Hills parking cars, my own voices of doubt began to chime in: *This is hopeless. You are wasting your time. You are never going to get back on that team.* It would have been so easy for me to walk away at that point, and no one would have blamed me. But during those moments of doubt, I ultimately chose faith in my deep-seated belief that God wanted me on that team for a purpose.

Training camp was due to begin the first week of August, and at the end of July, I was concerned about my lack of progress on Operation Intercept. I didn't have a playbook, a uniform, a locker, or even a gray practice T-shirt. But those few positive words uttered by Coach Carroll combined with that unwavering faith in a purpose cemented in my mind that it was only a matter of time until I was reinstated. In light of what I thought was my imminent return to the team, it made perfect sense to me that I should be in attendance at training camp.

I knew I would never get anywhere with Slutak without Coach Carroll's blessing, so I parked myself on that couch and waited for him. Sure enough, he came around the corner from his office, and I jumped up, blocking his path. Before I lost my nerve, I stuttered and stammered my way through asking, "Hey, I was hoping, like . . . Could I please . . . Is there any way I could be a part of training camp and be a part of the team?"

Coach's answer was delivered kindly yet firmly. "Oh, we don't have any space right now. Keep working hard."

I was crushed. While I appreciated his optimism, I was quickly realizing that the soft-hearted Carroll had difficulty saying no and was afraid to disappoint me, especially because he knew how hard I was working to get back on the team. It would've been far better for my emotions if he had been up front instead of stringing me along.

At my core, I was deeply ashamed of my predicament, and that shame drove me to isolation. I didn't dare process it with anyone because I was terrified to be seen as a failure. My friends, my family, and my teammates all thought I was still on the team. I was lying to all of them, and that deception was a staggering weight I carried with me every day. And to top it off, ever since April, I had been the unlikely underdog story everyone was talking about, reinforced by articles in *Sports Illustrated,* the *Los Angeles Times,* and the *Dallas Morning News,* along with features on CBS, ABC, and Fox Sports. They all thought I was still on the team too. Looking back, if I had chosen to share my burdens with a friend, maybe Mark or Beau, I could have experienced a measure of peace and freedom from the guilt and shame.

Each time someone asked me when I was going to be back playing football, my countenance sank a little lower and I dreaded the day I would be found out. Whenever I'd see a friend walking toward me, I'd start anticipating the conversation because it seemed like I had it multiple times per day.

"Hey, Ben, when are you going to be back on the field?" I'd get asked.

"Um, any day now," I'd reply, not wanting to look people in the eye for fear that they'd catch me in my lie.

The voices urging me to give up were getting louder and louder, and I wondered if my yearning to be on the team was really rooted in a divine purpose or a selfish pride. While I wouldn't find the answer to that particular question for several years, my desire was stronger than it ever had been.

Driven by desperation, I timidly approached Coach Carroll a few days later and hurriedly stumbled my way through a last-ditch proposition. "Could I please just sit in on the team meetings just so I can keep learning, then when my rehab is done, I'll be good to go?"

Coach Carroll seemed somewhat stunned by this latest request. Why in the world would a kid who had never played football, who had been carted off the field during spring training and undergone major shoulder surgery, who had been stripped of every piece of USC-issued football equipment, and who was slated for a nine-month recovery period think he had any right to make such a request? He took the course of least resistance and said, "Yeah, I guess, just only come to meetings and not to practice," obviously anxious to get on with his day. That was all I needed to hear, and as the rigorous training-camp schedule ramped up with six hours of football meetings per day, I made sure I arrived early and never missed a single one.

Based on the trainers' feedback, I knew I was progressing ahead of schedule. When I graduated from the training room to the weight room in early August, I sensed a touch of amazement on their part that I was able to make that jump significantly earlier than expected. My shoulder felt good, and it wasn't long before I was lifting even more than I had before my injury and had nearly recovered my full range of motion. So I began to apply the same type of persistent squeaky-wheel pressure to the training staff as I had to Coach Carroll. In mid-August, during one of my rehab sessions, I casually floated a trial balloon with Russ by saying, "So, Coach is ready to put me back on the team as soon as you release me." His response was immediate and definitive. "Whoa, whoa, whoa, it's only been four months since your surgery. You have a long way to go."

The next week I stubbornly prodded him again and suggested he schedule an appointment for me with Dr. Tibone to assess my progress, and once again he told me to back off. But by the third week, he knew I wasn't going to give up, and to placate me he got me on Dr. Tibone's schedule the following week.

The first home game on September 16 was against the Nebraska Cornhuskers, and I knew time was running out. I couldn't keep making excuses to my friends much longer. If I weren't at least standing on the sideline soon, the whole world would know I was a fraud.

On Monday of that week, I parked myself on the reception-area couch again. Coach Carroll seemed to have relaxed his guard a bit, and his responses had become somewhat more encouraging. That day I even thought I saw the corner of his mouth turn up in the beginning of that classic grin when he said, "This is great. We have some roster movement right now. If you get cleared by the doctor, maybe there will be a spot for you."

Although he offered absolutely no guarantee, I was so convinced of my purpose on the team that I boldly marched over to Slutak's office and confidently said, "Hey, I just talked to Coach, and he's pretty optimistic that I'll be back."

Slutak was in charge of the roster numbers, and the skeptical look on his face made it apparent that Coach Carroll hadn't discussed this with him. He said, "No, we don't have any roster spots." I stretched Coach's words once again by saying, "Well, Coach said that there might be some roster spots available, so I was wondering if I could just be on the sideline for the home game this weekend since I'm going to be back on the team."

He adamantly held his ground while shaking his head vigorously. "No, we can only have players currently on the team on the sideline, so unfortunately, we can't do that." His response was delivered with such an air of finality that I knew nothing I could say would change his mind. I was devastated. *What are my friends going to think if I'm not on the sideline for the first home game? They think I'm still on the team! What if they find out I'm not?*

And then the doubts began to rush in. *Maybe I don't have a chance. The season is already underway. It might be too late. How will I tell my friends that I've been lying to them all along? What about my purpose?*

It was going to feel foreign and humiliating to sit in the student section, since I hadn't been in one of those seats since my sophomore year. The line to get in that day was ridiculously long due to new security procedures, and I was worried about having to keep explaining why I wasn't on the sideline, so I quietly slipped away and walked home by myself. I sat in the living room and watched the game on television, which was the weirdest feeling for me because it was the first USC home game I hadn't seen from inside the Coliseum during my time as a student.

The Monday after the Nebraska game, my time had come, one way or another, as my appointment with Dr. Tibone was scheduled for that evening. Coach Carroll finally relented and said, "Ben, we have room on the roster, and you can officially rejoin the team as soon as you receive medical clearance." The trainers gave me their blessing and sprinkled a few more drops of water on my seedling of hope.

Even though I had felt a wave of momentum building over the last several weeks and the confidence in my God-given purpose on this team had become unshakable, I spent the entire day constantly pleading, *Please clear me. God, please clear me.* That night I nervously sat on Dr. Tibone's exam table. And after thoroughly examining my shoulder, pulling and prodding it, twisting and turning it while looking for any sign of instability or weakness, he gave me a puzzled look and asked, "When was your surgery?"

My reply of April 18 seemed to baffle him.

He checked his chart again as he slowly shook his head in disbelief and falteringly said, "I probably should not do this. In fact, I can't believe I am doing this, but you are cleared to play." I leaped off that table and took off like a running back with a clear path to the end zone to tell Slutak that I had been cleared. Judging from his less-than-enthusiastic reaction to my announcement, I wasn't sure he was convinced, or even in favor of Coach Carroll's decision, but he assured me that once everything had been confirmed by the trainers, I would be back on the field in time for practice the next day.

WALK ON
The Weight of Deception

The choice I made to deceive my friends about my standing on the team was a painful one. All my excuses boiled down to just one thing: my pride. At any point, I could have confided in a friend and would have received the support and affirmation I craved. Have you been carrying some type of deceit that is making you unsettled or miserable? What if you confessed it to God? And is there a friend you can share it with to clear your mind and your heart?

> All day long my disgrace is before me,
> and shame has covered my face.
>
> **—Psalm 44:15, ESV**

14

Second Chance

And just like that, I was back on the team. Although I thought the day I saw my name on the list taped to the door at Heritage Hall was the best day of my life, that day was nothing compared to this one.

All those days of rehab, beginning with lifting that very first light dumbbell to the teeth-gritting heavier weights and then enduring the painful stretching and range of motion exercises—it was all worth it. I floated down the stairway, feeling like the weight of a bruising 350-pound lineman had been lifted from my shoulders.

When I initially made the team, it was purely accidental; I never really felt as if I had earned it. Even after the rush of that holy moment on the steps when I realized I was on the team for a divine purpose, I could never escape the nagging feeling that I didn't really belong. But now, I was truly a full-fledged member of the 2006 Trojan football team and with that distinction came a certain amount of respect.

No longer was I a scrubby spring walk-on with only a sliver of hope for survival. Based on the research for my story, I knew how ridiculously long the odds were of the spring walk-ons still being on the team in the fall. Out of the nine walk-on players whose names had been on the list along with mine in March, only two were still on the fall roster. One was Lou Ferrigno Jr., a hulking six-foot-one, 230-pound linebacker who had been heavily recruited out of high school.

The other was me.

Slutak had obviously called ahead because when I got to the equipment room, Tino was waiting and had all my gear ready for me. When he told me he needed to assign me a new number, I meekly asked, "Do you think there is any way I could keep 24?"

He ran his stubby finger down the list on his clipboard, looked up, and said, "Yeah, we should be able to make that happen." I was stoked.

Having my old number back was extremely important to me. After all, 24 was the number I proudly pulled over my head on that first day of practice, and 24 was the number the trainers painstakingly stretched over my injured arm after I was humiliatingly carted off the field. And 24 was the number I was wearing in my dreams when I ran out of the tunnel at the Coliseum for the first time.

Making my way through the locker room, I found everything mostly as I had left it, with one notable and glorious exception: the athletic tape above my locker with my name scribbled on it was gone, and a brand-new cardinal placard with BEN MALCOLMSON #24 etched in gold was in its place.

Even though I had been faithfully attending the team meetings for more than a month, that afternoon's meeting felt different. The only person in the room who had any idea of the significance of this moment was Yogi. He said with a huge smile spread across his face, "I am so excited for you. Welcome back." He then added in a hushed tone with a note of seriousness, "If you need help with anything, you just let me know." I got a chuckle out of that because just a few weeks ago, he had been too busy to even acknowledge my existence. He had clearly forgiven me, and with the past behind us, we were buddies once again.

When he handed me my playbook, I paused for a moment. I remembered the first time I had held that precious playbook in my hands and the disgraceful day it had been stripped by Slutak when I feared it was the last time I would ever see it. Possessing the playbook symbolized my return, and holding it in my hands again felt empowering and life altering.

I was so excited for practice that afternoon. It was another perfect Southern California day, and while I took the walk to the practice field, as I had done more than a dozen times back in the spring, I felt changed. I had a much greater appreciation for this incredible opportunity and experienced a depth of gratitude that can only be gained after a loss.

My teammates didn't even give me a second look, since to them I was just another injured player who found his way back to the field. They had no idea what had transpired in the last five months or what a truly momentous day this was for me. I was absolutely giddy, running around the field with the exuberance of a ten-year-old on the playground after a long day cooped up in a classroom.

I cannot remember one drill, one play, one assignment, or one single thing that happened at practice that day except the aftermath of my first collision. I was lying on the ground, holding my breath, and wondering, *Am I okay? Did I hurt my shoulder again?* Once I realized I was fine, I jumped up with a mini fist pump. I experienced a type of exhilaration I hadn't even known was possible and wondered if I'd ever have a day that would make me feel this way again.

For the rest of the season, I actually welcomed those hits and faced every one with an attitude of "Bring it on! I'm back!" I honestly thought I was invincible and believed there was no way God was going to allow me to get hurt again.

As the season wore on, I threw myself out there with near reckless abandon, which resulted in multiple broken fingers, including several weeks where I was sporting one on each hand. I had so many bruises, I could hardly remember what my skin looked like when it wasn't mottled with a rainbow of black, blue, purple, and green. I practiced with broken ribs, wore braces on both ankles, and had a neck so stiff and sore that I had a hard time turning my head. I went to the training room every day to get ice on my shoulder, but I never complained about anything else. After all I had gone through, there was no way I was going to risk getting pulled out again.

Fall practice held an air of seriousness that hadn't been there in the spring. Fighting to climb to national-championship caliber was priority one, and Coach Carroll's mantra of Practice Is Everything took center stage on the field each afternoon.

To get a feel for how unique our practices were, you have to first understand the uniqueness of Coach Carroll. Growing up just outside San Francisco, he was a talented athlete in basketball and baseball, but football was his passion. Unfortunately, he wasn't big enough to make a run at an NFL career, and he has been ticked off about it ever since. So here he was some thirty years later, still fighting to keep that dream alive. He was really just a big kid who wanted to play football and loved to take part in practice, throwing passes and running around the field with unbridled joy until he was drenched with sweat. And that's why he always, always was willing to fuel another kid's dream and give him an opportunity to compete, even if he was too small or too inexperienced—or even if he was a student newspaper reporter.

He was also this crazy blend of creativity, competitiveness, and compassion, which reminded me of Willy Wonka from *Charlie and the Chocolate Factory*. Both come across as somewhat eccentric, possess boundless energy, and are never short on boyish mischievousness. And both are wildly entertaining—Coach Carroll loved to tickle the ivories or bust out a dance during a team meeting.

Coach Carroll's drive to be different was insatiable, and he likened his approach to Jerry Garcia's of the Grateful Dead, who said, "You do not merely want to be considered just the best of the best. You want to be considered the only ones who do what you do." That summarized Coach Carroll's practice philosophy perfectly. He wanted to create an environment for practice far different from anything else in existence. He repeatedly told us that practice was where "we made us," and that if we practiced really well, the game would take care of itself.

As a player, I found that mind-set extremely liberating. All we had to do was focus on practicing well and we were going to win on Saturday. Coach Carroll did such a great job of narrowing our focus to each moment of each day that we weren't even looking ahead to the next five minutes, let alone the game on Saturday. It was all about right here, right now. He created an environment where practice seemed more important than the game. Practice became a crucible, where instead of dreading it each day as I did as a kid, I wanted to compete, I wanted to win, and I wanted to show that I belonged.

Since I was still a bit of an outsider, I didn't have a bunch of close friends on the team. I struck up a somewhat unlikely friendship with Tyler Davis, our youngest quarterback. We were kind of an odd pair.

He was an eighteen-year-old freshman from Colorado with a wealth of football experience, and I was a twenty-one-year-old grad student who had learned nearly everything I knew about football in the last six months.

Tyler was always happy to improve his accuracy by throwing the ball around with me, and I loved to have him fire me passes near the sideline where I had to extend my arms and stretch my body out while dragging my toes to stay inbounds. That was so much fun for me because it made me feel like both a big-time wide receiver and a kid just playing catch in the park with my dad. Tyler and I connected on hundreds of those passes throughout the season, and I was grateful for our friendship.

I also loved spending time with our placekickers and punters, especially Mario Danelo and Taylor Odegard. While I remembered Mario's kindheartedness to me in the spring, I hadn't been around Taylor very much before my injury. Taylor was from Mercer Island, Washington, and although I didn't know it at the time, Taylor's friendship and Mercer Island would hold great significance for me in the future.

After seeing Mario's infectious smile at practice every day, I understood why he was known as the life of the party and deeply beloved by his teammates, his coaches, and his fans. His kindnesses to me continued, and while most of the guys hardly even acknowledged my existence, Mario went out of his way to make sure I was included. I would later come to realize that not only did Mario's care for me spring from his compassionate heart, but he also had firsthand experience of my struggle for acceptance. You see, he had been a walk-on himself in 2003, so he understood the pain of isolation that every new walk-on faces. And that's why oftentimes when I would be standing by myself on the sideline near the end of practice, I'd hear Mario calling out to me, "Hey, hey, Ben, come here. I want to tell you something." He never really had anything important to tell me, but it was his way of letting me know I had a friend.

Taylor and Mario were the class clowns of our team and virtually inseparable. In fact, they were so close that it was almost impossible to imagine one without the other.

WALK ON
God of Second Chances

When I found myself miraculously back on the team, I was filled with a fresh sense of gratitude and appreciation. God is indeed the God of second chances. How has God offered you a second chance when you were in a situation where you had given up hope?

> But this I call to mind,
>   and therefore I have hope:
> The steadfast love of the LORD never ceases;
>   his mercies never come to an end;
> they are new every morning;
>   great is your faithfulness.
>
> **—Lamentations 3:21–23, ESV**

15

Get Ben In

My dream of running out of the Coliseum tunnel was almost within reach, and I simply could not wait for that day to come. As if I wasn't building it up enough in my head, all my friends kept asking, "Aren't you excited to be suited up on the sideline?" Since they had no idea I had been living a lie throughout my injury, none of them could even begin to imagine the complete relief and absolute elation I felt.

October 7 was the day I had been anticipating for months, and I climbed into the fancy coach bus for the short ride to the Coliseum with a heart brimming with joy. Except for the growl of the diesel engine, the bus ride was completely quiet, with each of us sitting alone listening to music and lost in his own thoughts. The buses drove bumper to bumper, like a parade of elephants traveling tail to trunk with barely three feet between them. Traffic had been completely stopped for us on the 110, so we were the only moving vehicles on the highway for the entire three-mile trip to the Coliseum. We looked like part of a presidential motorcade.

After we rolled up to the Coliseum, we entered the famed Trojan Walk with Coach Carroll in the lead. Of all the storied traditions at

USC, this became one of my favorites. The Trojan Walk is essentially a five-foot-wide, cordoned-off pathway, with fans lined up twenty deep to create a roaring human tunnel amidst shouts of "Fight on!" There were fans of all ages and stages, from USC alums to students and tons of little kids, some hoisted on shoulders and some on all fours reaching through their parents' legs and waving their hands for a high five from one of the players.

It was really too much to take in at once: the sound, the color, the rush. It felt like being ushered down the red carpet at the Academy Awards, and it took place every time we had a home game.

At the end of the Trojan Walk, the large wrought-iron gates of the Coliseum swung open, and almost immediately we went from the commotion of a rock concert to the silence of a cemetery. I found myself dwarfed in the shadow of the iconic peristyle, a massive series of stone columns showcasing a fifty-foot arch in the center with the cauldron from the 1984 Olympics rising from its top. The inside of the arch was lined with a stone mosaic of the sun, highlighted with glittering gold accents. It was all so grand and glorious, and I felt so small and insignificant. Standing under that arch and looking out over the ninety-two thousand empty seats reflecting the brilliant California sun was absolutely mesmerizing. It's not like I had never been inside the Coliseum before, but today, through the eyes of a player, everything looked different.

Coach Carroll revered the Coliseum and would often tell us stories about the epic battles that were fought there, reinforcing the idea that if we wanted to be great, we had to be dominant at home. And when he gathered us together at the top of the steps, his voice rang out, "What an amazing day today! This is our home. Let's protect it. Let's make the most of it. Here we go."

We then gathered at midfield for a simple prayer, and the booming "Amen" of a hundred guys echoed through the empty stadium as
if we were in Saint Paul's Cathedral in London. From there, we
headed up to the locker room, through the one-hundred-yard-long,
fifty-foot-wide, cardinal concrete tunnel of my dreams. I was stunned
by the absolute uniformity of the equipment in the locker room. It
looked as if our equipment managers had been trained by the US
Navy to make the entire room, from the ceiling all the way down to
the spotless carpet, look shipshape. The helmets were polished so
they gleamed like garnets, while the gold pants, the gray gloves, and
even the socks looked like they were brand new. I was almost afraid
to touch anything.

When I saw my pads sitting on the shelf in my locker, I was
thrilled to see that my jersey had already been stretched over them.
The back of my jersey with my "24" reminded me of the hundred-
year-old USC tradition to have the jersey display only your number
and not your name. The significant point is that no player is more
important than another, and it's all about the team.

After our pregame warm-ups, I could feel the excitement beginning to build. We raced from the field all the way up to the locker
room. Our thunderous screams and shouts filled the tunnel with a
deafening roar as we barreled past the opponents' locker room and
reminded them that this was our home. As game time approached,
the older guys started pulling everyone together, and it was almost as
if someone was steadily turning an invisible volume knob, trans-
forming the center of the locker room into a mosh pit with guys
dancing, bouncing around on the balls of their feet, hollering, and
working themselves into a near frenzy. I was self-conscious and try-

ing to stay under the radar, so on the outside I was just sort of sway-ing side to side, but on the inside I was spinning like the teacups at Disneyland.

The cry went up, "Trojans on three—one, two, three, TROJANS!" It took a while for a hundred wild-eyed guys to squeeze out of the single doorway, but soon we were all standing in the tunnel and things were reaching a fever pitch. I had never been in the tunnel before a game, so I had no idea what was about to happen. Guys lined up in groups that spanned the width of the tunnel, locked arms, and slowly and methodically began to walk down the tunnel while chanting in unison, "War time, war time."

The acoustics in the tunnel were unique, and with the steady, deep baritone chants, our voices bounced off the walls, barraging us from all directions. Between the rhythmic *clickety-clack* of our metal cleats on the concrete and the reverberating echoes of our chants, the air pulsed with electricity.

When we reached the bottom of the tunnel, we fired one an-other up with high fives and helmet smacks as we waited for the booming voice of the announcer. "*Heeere* come the Trojans!" We swarmed onto the field in one giant blur of cardinal and gold. With guys running in several different directions, I wasn't sure where I was supposed to go, but I saw a group of guys kneeling in the end zone to pray so I ran down to join them. *Wow, thank You, God. This is amazing. You've brought me here. Thank You.*

This was the first time I had ever seen a game from field level, and I quickly realized that I couldn't really *see* anything, but I could *feel* a tremendous amount of energy swirling around me. I could hear the *thwack* of the ball when it passed from the center into the ready hands of J. D. Booty, our quarterback. His "Check, check!" at the line came through loud and clear as well as the sickening *thud*s when bodies clashed, followed by the usual moans and groans.

As the first half ended, the entire team bolted up the tunnel to the locker room. With the coaches yelling, "All the way up, all the way up," we blew past our opponents, who were trudging along toward their locker room.

I was overjoyed to see a table piled high with icy-cold bottles of Gatorade and loads of protein bars in the locker room. The butterflies that had filled my nervous stomach from the moment I woke up had been completely annihilated by my adrenaline, and I was starving. I ripped off those wrappers like a kid at Halloween, stuffing the bars into my mouth and chasing them down with gulps of Gatorade.

The coaches were chattering so fast, scribbling furiously on whiteboards, using sloppy Xs and lopsided Os and all sorts of squiggly lines. I was completely lost. The rest of the guys were clearly dialed in, nodding their heads, but without my playbook in front of me, they may as well have been speaking Greek. My head was spinning, and before I knew it, Coach Carroll was giving a rah-rah speech and shouting, "Trojans on three—one, two, three, TROJANS!" We went through the same drill again: squeeze a hundred supersweaty guys out of the doorway, lock arms, and march down the tunnel chanting, "War time, war time."

At the end of the third quarter, we were up 23–13, but it still felt too close for comfort. Mario had already kicked three field goals, en route to an individual game record of four field goals. But in the fourth quarter, Washington scored a touchdown, which cut our lead to just three points, 23–20. With 1:34 left in the game, Mario nailed a 21-yard field goal to increase our lead to six points. But six points is a precarious lead in a football game, as the other team can tie the score with a single play. Washington had the ball and started driving, making one first down after another. My journalistic instincts understood the magnitude of what was happening: we hadn't lost at home since 2001, a streak that was twenty-eight games at that point.

In the past, I would have been salivating at that juicy headline, but the thought that our win streak was now in jeopardy at my first game was horrifying. I could still hear Coach Carroll's emphatic charge to us before the game: "We gotta be dominant at home. We gotta be dominant at home." And just like that, the clock ran out on Washington's last-gasp comeback attempt, and the game was over. We won! The postgame scene in the locker room was rowdy, with guys hooting and hollering and jumping around while belting out the USC fight song as if they had never won a game before.

As adrenaline charged as the game had been, I knew the sideline was the closest I was ever going to get to any real action, and I was completely content with that. Well, that is until one of my fraternity brothers, Mike Escoto, asked me a question that would change everything.

"What do you mean you don't care if you get to play in a game?"

I shrugged my shoulders and replied, "I really don't."

He was clearly miffed. He leaned toward me and playfully whispered, "C'mon, Ben, let's be honest here."

I conceded that there was perhaps a sliver of desire and followed up with a slice of reality. "That would be cool, but I'm really happy just practicing during the week and running out of the tunnel on Saturdays." After all, simply being a part of the heralded USC football program was still a really big deal, especially for someone like me, who had spent years documenting the great accomplishments of other athletes.

He started fanning the flame by pulling my other fraternity brothers into the conversation and saying, "Hey, guys, Ben doesn't even want to play," and then added with a high-pitched squawk, "Isn't that ridiculous?"

I knew he was trying to ruffle my feathers and was going to keep ruffling until I gave in, so I agreed, "Of course I'd like to get in a game."

Mike was affectionately known as the Kung Fu Panda around the house. Just like Po, he was beloved, playful, and fast talking, and we never underestimated his ability to make things happen. He had been a member of the fraternity for years, but due to some personal circumstances, he had to take a couple of years off from attending USC. Upon his return, he became our chief cook, and with a true servant's heart, he made the meals for forty ravenous college guys three times a day. I had an understanding of some of the challenges Mike had faced and took every opportunity I could to make sure he knew how much we loved and appreciated him. Although I didn't know it at the time, my desire to come alongside him as a friend meant a great deal to him.

Besides his ability to dish up a mouthwatering chicken marsala and pack the perfect sack lunch, he had a wealth of other talents, one of which was campaign organization. He had worked on a wide variety of campaigns, from creating a slogan for a house manager to hitting the trail for a local politician at election time. He also held a deep reverence for USC football and celebrated with me when I made the team, agonized with me over the heartbreak of my injury, and was one of my biggest cheerleaders as I battled my way through rehab. I had seen how consumed Mike could become about something he believed in. Once his passions were stirred by a cause, look out. So when he chose me as the object of his next campaign, I should have known I was in for a wild ride.

In just a few hours, Mike was busy creating some artwork that would be the cornerstone of his "Get Ben In" campaign. The background was a fading gradient of gold to cardinal and had my name prominently displayed across the top. Below my name, in a smaller italicized font, it read, "As Featured in *Sports Illustrated,* the *Los Angeles Times,* and the *Daily Trojan.*"

Below that subheading in bold black letters was "This storybook needs an ending. As fans, let's help this walk-on live his dream and get into a game. If we're going to win and it's late in the fourth quarter, let the Trojan Nation know that we want number 24 in the game by chanting, 'Get Ben in!'" And to the left of the text was a picture of me running in midstride at practice.

Before the night was over, Mike had placed his first order with Vista Print for postcards to be delivered later that week. And when he handed me that first card, I was astonished. Along with the cards, he also created a black-and-white flyer and started printing batches at the Kinko's a block away when he had the cash to pay for them.

At that time, I had no idea how "astonished" would become "jaw dropping" as Mike ramped up his campaign and enlisted an army of USC students and supporters to fight for my cause in the weeks to come.

By the time our game against Oregon on November 11 rolled around, Mike's "Get Ben In" campaign was gaining some traction. He rallied a group of guys to pass out the cards and staple the flyers

on the twenty hexagonal message boards around campus that adver-
tised everything from calculus lessons to yoga classes. Instead of
tacking up one flyer on each board, they plastered over *all* the other
flyers on *all* six sides of the message boards, so nothing was visible
but the "Get Ben In" message.

And in addition to the student army, Mike was also gaining re-
inforcements from other sources. My parents had gotten wind of
what was going on and wanted to be involved, so one afternoon
several large cardboard boxes were delivered to the fraternity, con-
taining five hundred cardinal T-shirts with four-inch gold block let-
tering across the front that read GET BEN IN and a large gold "24"
centered on the back. Our living room turned into a distribution
center of sorts, with my friends and other random people showing up
and asking for a T-shirt. As I watched this start to mushroom, I
wondered, *Holy cow, what in the world is going on here?*

Not satisfied with just USC and my family, Mike decided it was
time to implement an international strategy. One night, he called me
to his room and said, "Hey, Ben, come here. I want to show you
something." He pulled up his computer screen and proceeded to
describe the various components of the GetBenIn.com website he
had created to increase the reach of the campaign. It featured the
same graphic as the cards and had several tabs, for media, students,
and a place for people to send in comments about how my story had
inspired them. I stared at him, smiled, and slowly shook my head in
disbelief. "This is crazy. *You* are crazy. Why are you doing this?"

"Ben, you know me. I love doing crazy things," Mike said.
"You've been there for me, and now I want to be there for you. Plus,
this is really fun. You'll be USC's Rudy."

As time went on, my story took on a much deeper significance

than just me making the team. It became a message of hope for anyone who was facing a seemingly impossible situation. There were
countless messages sent via the website from people who had heard
my story and wanted to encourage me.

Two of those messages in particular meant a great deal to me.
One was from a seventeen-year-old who had tried out for her high
school volleyball team three years straight but had never made the
roster. As a senior, she had decided to skip the tryouts because she
could not face the possibility of failing again. But after reading my
story, she was inspired to give it one more try—and she made it. And
the other was from Pfc. Ronald Curtis and a battalion of football-
loving soldiers who were stationed in Iraq. "Your story is just one
more reason why we're doing what we're doing over here. Thank you
for reminding us what hope can really do for people. We've never
been so proud to be Americans as we continue to bring hope to the
Iraqis. Thank you for bringing hope and a little bit of joy and excitement to us."

Having this much attention was terribly uncomfortable for me
since I had spent most of my life trying to stay backstage and avoid
the spotlight. I was particularly embarrassed when a coach or teammate suggested I might have had a hand in instigating any of this.
One day Coach Carroll asked, "What's with this 'Get Ben In' thing?
Are you doing that? Are you putting up signs everywhere trying to
get into a game?"

I was mortified and quickly denied any involvement, "No, no,
it's not me, Coach, I swear." Or the time Yogi told me that he saw
"Get Ben In" stuff "everywhere around campus." But even in the
face of my embarrassment, my friends' heartfelt efforts, especially
Mike's, made me feel completely humbled and honored.

On November 11, kickoff for the Oregon game was scheduled for 7:28 p.m. under the bright lights at the Coliseum. I was up early since I couldn't sleep, and one of my fraternity brothers teasingly said with a chuckle, "You might want to check out campus today." My first thought was, *Oh no, what have they done?*

Since I had a bunch of time to kill and I knew the hours would crawl by before game time, I decided to walk over and investigate. Nothing could have prepared me for what I was about to see.

During the night, Mike and his band of merry men had descended upon the campus, intent on taping, stapling, and otherwise covering every possible exposed surface they could find. Not only were the flyers plastered over the entirety of every message board; they were also wallpapered on every trash can across campus. There were stacks of cards in every hallway and classroom, and cards were scattered upon every tabletop. This was no joke anymore. It had turned into an all-out blitz. I felt very loved and respected by the campaign, and their efforts moved me and made me realize that this story was far bigger than me.

While the bus ride that afternoon, the locker room, and the tunnel were all the same for this Oregon matchup, there was one marked difference after the kickoff, and that was the sea of cardinal shirts in the student section intermittently chanting, "Get Ben in! Get Ben in!"

The chants were fairly isolated, and I was hoping no one on the field could hear them, but some of my teammates started ribbing me, saying, "Do you hear that?" And I was thinking, *Um, this is really awkward. There are lots of other guys who deserve to play way more than me.* The game wasn't really close. We were ahead 14–0 at the

half and 28–3 at the end of the third quarter. Oregon scored a touchdown in the fourth, and we answered right back with a touchdown
of our own and were leading 35–10, when we got the ball back on
the 5-yard line backed up against our own end zone.

Reserve guys had been subbed in for the entire fourth quarter,
but since my name hadn't been called, I had accepted the fact that
this wasn't going to be my night. With only fourteen seconds to play,
one of the reserve wide receivers came out of the game, and I heard
tight ends coach Brennan Carroll excitedly call my name. "Benny,
you're in!"

I had a long forty-five yards to run from where I was standing on
the sideline all the way to the end zone, and I covered that distance
like an Indy car heading for the checkered flag. By the time I got to
the huddle, the clock was already running and the quarterback,
Mark Sanchez, was rushing everyone to the line while shouting,
"Let's go! Let's go! We've gotta get Ben in." While the guys were
scrambling, Sanchez was pleading with the ref, "Please let us get this
play off." The ref was apologetically shrugging his shoulders while
saying, "I can't do anything. The clock is running."

And run it did. All the way down to 0:00 right before we could
snap the ball.

My first reaction was *Oh no, I didn't get my play.* Then in an
instant, quicker than that clock ran out, I thought about how cool it
was that I was actually standing on the field with my teammates.
Mark immediately approached me and said, "I'm so sorry. I was trying so hard." I was incredibly touched by his response and the fact
that he was even mindful of giving me that opportunity.

We got so close.

The next home game was a nationally televised matchup against the California Golden Bears on November 18 with a 5:13 p.m. kickoff. The fans wearing their "Get Ben In" T-shirts were loud in the student section, but the game was terrifically tight, and there wasn't an opportunity for many of the reserve players to take the field.

The last home game was on November 25, when number-three-ranked USC would be taking on sixth-ranked Notre Dame in the classic rivalry game. The buildup to the game was intensified because it was senior night—all the seniors received a special pregame recognition—and while the athletic department was gearing up for an unforgettable evening, Mike was pouring accelerant on the "Get Ben In" campaign as well. He had reprinted the postcards multiple times, and bigger and flashier posters had replaced the simple flyers. Having distributed more than ten thousand cards and a thousand posters over the last three weeks, his all-out campus barrage continued.

Knowing that this game was my last chance, he was getting even bolder and putting posters in places that were frowned upon, prompting a visit from a university representative asking him to back off a bit. Mike had been monitoring the website as well as posting on every online message board he could find, and he had been in touch with several national media outlets, urging them to cover my story.

And four days before the game, he actually had the audacity to crash the USC football press conference. Technically, he didn't really crash the press conference. He just walked right in as if he belonged there, helped himself to the sumptuous buffet, and wedged his little portable recorder in the bank of microphones alongside those from ESPN, *Sports Illustrated, Los Angeles Times,* and the rest of the big boys. Then he patiently kept raising his hand and waiting for his turn to ask Coach Carroll his question. Near the very end, his opportunity finally came.

Sandwiched between a question on Dwayne Jarrett's injury and Desmond Reed's recovery, Mike was called upon and boldly asked Coach Carroll, "Do you plan to play all of the seniors on senior day?" Coach Carroll clearly wasn't expecting that question and bounced around a bit while trying to answer it. He affirmed that he would *like* to do that but said that it was "more difficult than you'd think." He emphasized that the recognition of running out of the tunnel and the tribute of the former players was what really separated this game from others. But his closing comment was, "I hope everybody can have a chance to play, though."

At the conclusion of the press conference, sports information director Tim Tessalone made a beeline for Mike and politely, although clearly perturbed, asked, "How did you get in here?"

To which Mike calmly answered, "I just walked in."

Tessalone continued authoritatively, "Well, this isn't how this usually works. You are supposed to check in with someone."

And then, with narrowed eyes and a suspicious look on his face, he asked, "Hey, aren't you the guy with all the flyers?" He added a stern note of caution: "You need to watch where you are putting those flyers." Little did Tessalone know that it was Mike's goal to make sure *every single one* of the thirty-two thousand students at USC was aware of the "Get Ben In" campaign, and I think he came close to achieving it.

The buzz around campus was definitely increasing, and people were beginning to recognize me. Everywhere I went complete strangers approached me and excitedly asked, "Are you 'Get Ben In'? We're cheering for you!"

And it came as no surprise that Yogi was my biggest fan as he steadfastly championed my cause. All week he told me, "I'm really, really pushing to get you in. I'm already planting seeds and want to make it happen." With my parents, my grandparents, and my brother all flying in for the game, I forced myself to temper my expectations and went about the week with a business-as-usual attitude, not allowing myself to get my hopes up.

But there really was no escape from the national hype surrounding this game, with many expecting it to be even better than the year before, which had been a thriller to say the least. Between the raucous rivalry and the fact that ESPN's *College GameDay* had selected this as one of the biggest matchups of the season, it was bound to be a spectacle in every sense of the word.

A year earlier I had covered the fantastic USC–Notre Dame game, a matchup that has been referred to by many as the "game of the century." After watching most of the game from the press box at Notre Dame Stadium, I headed down to the field along with the other reporters for the last five minutes.

It was an epic back-and-forth battle when Notre Dame took the lead with just over two minutes left to play, 31–28. The Trojans miraculously converted a fourth-and-9, and then a few plays later Matt Leinart fumbled the ball out of bounds at the 1-yard line. Even though the rules state that a fumble out of bounds results in a stopped clock, the scoreboard clock continued to run. The moment it hit 0:00, the Notre Dame student section rushed the field, and I was nearly trampled by the stampeding students. The officials determined that in actuality there were still seven seconds left in the game, and when the PA announcer asked everyone to return to the seats, I was relieved I had survived the madness and that the Trojans would have a chance to rewrite the end of their story.

It took a few minutes for security to clear the field as the Trojans huddled up to discuss their last possession. When the clock started again, Coach Carroll appeared to be signaling from the sideline for Leinart to spike the ball, which would allow the kicking unit to set up for a field goal and potentially tie the game. But Carroll's signal was a decoy, and Leinart made the decision to go for the touchdown. That's when USC running back Reggie Bush channeled all of his two hundred pounds into pushing Leinart into the end zone, a play that would come to be known as the Bush Push.

And just like that, the hullabaloo of 80,795 fans turned to heartbreak as they froze in stunned silence. Victory had been snatched from their hands, and now the Trojans were celebrating like the Irish had been just moments before.

Since I knew firsthand what this iconic rivalry was all about, I knew Notre Dame's team and fans would show up at the Coliseum hungry for revenge. And I also knew that their hunger would probably devour any chance I might have to take the field. So I vowed to enjoy senior night and be grateful for my spot on the sideline. The success of my season didn't hinge upon getting a chance to play—in my eyes, I had already achieved success because of what I had overcome to now be a part of the team—but I was concerned about the tremendous disappointment my friends and family would feel after all they had invested in the "Get Ben In" campaign.

Along with my excited eagerness for senior night, I received some unexpected news during the week that ramped up my anticipation even more. Every Thursday a list was posted outside the equipment room with the names of players on the travel squad, who would either be making the trip to an away game or staying at the team hotel the night before a home game.

Since the list was arranged alphabetically, it was easy to make a quick scan each week to see if my name was on it. I knew I was *never* going to be on it, but like a lottery player who buys a ticket every week just in case, I peeked at the list on Thursdays just to be sure. When I casually glanced over it that week, zeroing in on the *M*'s, I thought I saw my name on the list. I looked around to make sure no one was watching, did a double take, and confirmed that yes, my name was definitely on the list. It was a huge moment for me because it signified that I had really made it as a member of the team. It was the coolest thing in the world.

After our light practice that Friday evening, we took a bus to the Marriott where the final team meetings were conducted. Coach Carroll delivered a homily that would rival any energetic preacher's as he talked about how much he revered and respected the opportunity to play on national television and how much he loved the guys in the room. He closed with a simple reminder: "Nothing's different for us. We are playing at the Coliseum, and the field is still 100 yards long and 53 1/3 yards wide."

I woke up extra early the next morning, propped myself up in that luxurious bed, surrounded by four big, fluffy pillows, and turned on ESPN's *College GameDay*. I watched it nearly every week and got a kick out of seeing Chris Fowler, Kirk Herbstreit, Lee Corso, and Desmond Howard banter back and forth with all those crazy college students waving their signs behind them. The peristyle of the Coliseum, bathed in morning sunshine with the gorgeous blue sky behind it, was the backdrop on that particular morning, and over the left shoulders of Chris Fowler and Desmond Howard I couldn't believe what I saw.

There were two enormous seven-foot GET BEN IN! signs, featuring life-sized photos of me, bobbing up and down to catch the eye of the cameraman. When I recognized Mike and my brother, Clay, wearing their "Get Ben In" T-shirts, as the ones holding them, I was absolutely dumbstruck.

I just sat there, laughing and staring in amazement at the television, knowing full well that if I was seeing this, so were my teammates, my friends, my coaches, and hundreds of thousands of other people across the country.

We finished a final walk-through and meal at the hotel and then loaded onto the waiting buses.

Upon arrival at the Coliseum, I entered the Trojan Walk and went down the steps to the field for the last time. I lingered in the locker room for a minute, knowing I would never be there again and thought about how grateful I was for all the memories from the season. We did our "war time" chant all the way down the tunnel, but since it was senior night, instead of the announcer introducing us as a team, the seniors were introduced individually and ran out of the tunnel one by one. Right before I was introduced, Coach Carroll, beaming, shook my hand and gave me a hug. I was so overwhelmed that I felt dizzy.

Since I was the scrubbiest of all the seniors, my name was called first. As "Ben Malcolmson, number 24, from Dallas, Texas" boomed over the PA system, I ran onto the field through a gauntlet of friends, family, and alumni. Everything rushed toward me in a blur of noise and color and excitement. About halfway through my run, I pointed up at the student section as if to say, "This is for you!" Since it was dark and they were so far away, I couldn't really see them, but I knew they were there, cheering me on and proudly wearing their "Get Ben In" shirts.

The game was fairly close through the first three quarters, and I abandoned any snippet of hope that had been hiding in my heart to take the field. In the fourth quarter, USC broke the game wide open and went on a scoring streak, starting with a field goal by Mario, which made the score 31–17. Then with 8:21 left on the clock, we scored a touchdown to push our lead to 37–17. Notre Dame answered right back with a touchdown of their own to make the score 37–24 with 3:39 left to play. Notre Dame then attempted an onside kick that was somehow recovered by USC's Brian Cushing and returned for a touchdown, which was virtually unheard of; we were repeatedly coached to field an onside kick and down it immediately.

I will always believe a divine hand orchestrated that miraculous turn of events. We were now up 44–24, and Notre Dame started their last drive with 3:31 on the clock. After one first down, they went into their hurry-up offense, which ended on a failed fourth-down conversion, and the ball was turned over to us on downs.

With only 1:49 left on the clock, the flurry of activity around me seemed to be ramping up by the second. That snippet of hope grew exponentially with each tick of the clock. I could hear the "Get Ben in!" chants now, loud and clear, from pockets all over the stadium, not just the student section. I put my helmet on so I looked ready, just in case I got the call. And then I slowly began inching down into that zone I had been afraid to enter for the entire season: the mob of coaches and hopeful subs on the sideline in close proximity to the play.

And then, just like in the Oregon game a few weeks before, tight ends coach Brennan Carroll turned to me and excitedly shouted, "Benny, you're in!" *Oh boy, here we go. This is it!*

You would think when the moment I had been waiting for all season finally arrived I would have sprung into action and known exactly what to do. I was standing on the sideline near the 50, and the offense was getting ready to huddle up on the hash mark around the 30, so I had about forty yards to cover in order to reach them. I was trucking as fast as I could possibly go, but those few seconds felt like a few minutes. I could not hear anything at that point; the entire stadium, or even the whole city of Los Angeles, could have been chanting, and I would not have heard them. It was just a loud, steady hum buzzing around in my helmet, and the culmination of my last seven months and seven days had come down to this moment.

Thankfully, there was one spot in the huddle that was open, or who knows how long I would have run in circles as if I was playing duck, duck, goose. I arrived just in time to hear quarterback Mark Sanchez call the play, "I-right Victory on one. Ready. Break!" Mark turned to me and said, "Ben, we got you. We got you!"

Meanwhile, I was downright frantic. *I-right Victory on one, I-right Victory on one—what does that even mean? Oh crap, where am I supposed to go? What am I supposed to do? We never practiced this! That was not in the playbook!!* I was freaking out and trying to think, but I couldn't think that fast. I remembered him saying something about "right" and I thought I was a Z, but I wasn't sure anymore. Deciding it was best to act like a Z and picturing what a victory formation looked like on film, I moved toward the right side and lined up close to our tight end. I got down in my stance and looked across the line at the Notre Dame cornerback wearing that legendary shiny gold helmet. Right before I heard Mark's cadence and the snap of the ball, I thought, *This is it! I can't believe this!*

After Mark had taken a knee, I vaguely remembered I was supposed to protect the quarterback, so I ran over in his direction. I instinctively raised my left arm in a fist-pump celebration. I had gotten into a game. "Get Ben In" had become a success. (The funny thing is, I later found out that I lined up incorrectly and should have been penalized five yards. I'm forever grateful that the officials didn't throw a flag on me!)

The next few minutes were even more of a blur. An ABC cameraman and reporter approached me almost immediately and asked me how it felt to finally get in the game and see the "Get Ben In" campaign come to fruition. I went over to the stands and took photos with my family. Yogi was waiting for me when I returned to the locker room and wrapped me in a big bear hug as he proudly exclaimed, "You got in! You got in!"

Coach gave his postgame celebratory speech right before the entire team broke into a raucous rendition of the fight song. And there I was in the back corner, floating and overwhelmed with an indescribable joy.

My phone was maxed out with voice mails and text messages, most with the same three words: "Ben got in!" But there was one voice mail I will never forget. Bob Yates, the sports editor at the *Dallas Morning News,* who had delivered the devastating news back in March that he did not have a job for me, left a touching message: "Ben, I am so proud of you. I will never forget the image of you holding that fist pump for the rest of my life."

To think that if I had gotten the job at the *Dallas Morning*

News, I would not have been standing in that locker room. I would have missed the highest and the lowest days of my life. And I was reminded that none of this was a coincidence. Even when I was discouraged, even when I felt lost, and even when I had nearly lost hope, the hand of God had been carefully coaching me through every play of my life, even those that weren't in the playbook.

WALK ON
Be Like Mike

The Get Ben In campaign orchestrated by Mike was an incredible gift of friendship that I will never forget. It made me feel treasured and loved. Who in your life can you be a "Mike" to? By encouraging and bringing joy into the lives of others, we are always the ones who are most blessed.

Therefore encourage one another and build
one another up, just as you are doing.

—1 Thessalonians 5:11, ESV

16

Be a Light

My fist-pumping elation was soon overshadowed by yet another series of disappointments. In the quest to discover my purpose earlier in the season, I felt a nudge to spearhead a team Bible study, so I asked Slutak if I could use a meeting room before practice on Fridays at 1:30 p.m. I spent hours poring over my Bible searching for the perfect passage, wrote out the entire study word for word in my notebook, and even created a few discussion questions. I printed a hundred flyers and passed them out to my teammates, surprising myself with my boldness. Normally I was hesitant to talk about my faith, especially in a secular environment like a college football locker room. But I was so sure God was going to pack the house with my teammates and maybe even build this Bible study into a long-standing Trojan football tradition.

I arrived fifteen minutes early and moved the plastic chairs with the fold-down desks from their usual row-by-row formation into a circle. And then I sat and waited and prayed while staring at the historic pictures of wide receivers from the eighties hanging catawampus on the cardinal-colored wall. Filled with so much confidence and enthusiasm, I nearly jumped out of my seat when the door opened at 1:28 p.m.—*finally!* A teammate popped his head in and asked, "What's going on in here?" When I told him we were having a Bible study, he replied, "Oh cool," and promptly left.

My eyes became glued to the face of the clock mounted above the door as the second hand seemed to mock me: *tick, tick, tick. No one's coming. Tick, tick, tick. No one's coming.* After fifteen minutes, I realized the clock was right. No one was going to show up. I packed up my Bible and notebook and buried them in my backpack along with a hefty weight of disappointment. And I carried that discouragement everywhere I went for the next couple of weeks, along with a backbreaking burden of doubt and defeat. I felt like a complete failure. I was trying to follow what I sensed as God's direction. *Couldn't You have sent just one guy to my Bible study?*

Even though I was still passionate about finding my purpose, I was hesitant to put myself out there again. But about a month later, toward the middle of the season, I felt another nudge that I was meant to lead a prayer group instead of a Bible study. The feeling was so intense, I wondered how I could have missed it the first time. Armed with a renewed sense of confidence and enthusiasm, I reformatted the flyers, gave them to my teammates, reserved the room, arrived fifteen minutes early, rearranged the chairs, and sat and waited and prayed with the *tick, tick, tick* pounding in my ears.

No one showed up.

How could I possibly have missed my purpose again? I felt like a miserable failure once more.

Although I had been burned twice, the fire in my soul continued to spark, and I became captivated by a passage in the book of

Matthew in which Jesus tells His followers, "Let your light shine before others" (5:16, NIV). And then it hit me! I was making this too complicated. Just as I had done when I was sports editor, I became so focused on what I was supposed to do that I had forgotten who I was supposed to be. My purpose was simply to *be* a light in the lives of my teammates. Lights don't really *do* anything. They don't have to create events or facilitate gatherings; they just shine. So fulfilling my purpose meant just being a light on that team. My presence was my purpose.

The weight of disappointment tumbled from my shoulders. And over the next few weeks, I tried to connect more intentionally with my teammates and coaches. But practice and school were all consuming, leaving very little free time to invest in relationship building, and frankly, no one seemed the least bit interested.

At this point, my soul had been scorched, and I was completely perplexed about my purpose. Football season was almost over. Time was running out. The promise of my purpose was seriously in question. Every time I had been completely convinced that I was following God's lead, and every time it appeared I had been way off course. I directed my frustration heavenward and emphasized the urgency of my situation. *If I have a purpose, You've got one month, so You better get going. What are You waiting for?*

In light of the last three devastating failures, to say I was reluctant to continue the search for my purpose was an understatement. I didn't think I could survive another round of disappointment. So when I felt a nudge after reading a verse in the Bible, I didn't exactly jump on it immediately. I let the nudge kind of stir around a bit in my mind before allowing Isaiah 55:11 to take hold: "So is my word that goes out from my mouth: It will not return to me empty, but will accomplish what I desire and achieve the purpose for which I sent it" (NIV).

Try as I might, I couldn't shake the feeling that those words held a message for me. There was no denying it. And when I quit resisting, it was as if a lightning bolt from heaven reignited the fire of purpose in my soul. I knew "the word" referred to the Bible, and the message to me was undeniable. Every one of my teammates needed to receive a Bible.

My grandfather had recently begun volunteering for Gideons International, the group that passes out Bibles in hotel rooms and on college campuses. I called him immediately. My grandmother answered the phone, and before she could even say, "Hello," I blurted out, "Is there any way Poppy could give me a hundred Bibles from the Gideons?" She sweetly called him to the phone, and after I explained what I needed, he wasn't very encouraging. He said, "Benny, the Gideons don't typically take on projects like that. But I'll tell you what, I'll make some calls and see if I can help you." To my delight, they called back the next morning and told me that the Bibles were being shipped to the fraternity house. I assumed that the Gideons were donating the Bibles; it wasn't until many years later that I discovered my grandparents had footed the bill.

I was so absolutely sure, so fully convinced *this* was my purpose that the idea of another failure never entered my mind. *This is it! I know it!* When the Bibles arrived in five large, heavy cardboard boxes, I lugged them up the stairs to my room and decided not to tell anyone what I was doing because I didn't want to make a big deal out of it or answer any questions from my fraternity brothers. And because I was so beaten down by my failed previous attempts to share my faith with my teammates, I especially didn't want any of them to know, so I planned to keep the whole project under wraps.

I decided the Bibles would make perfect Christmas gifts, so I typed up a note that read "The greatest Christmas gift you will ever receive—the gift of Jesus Christ." I added the USC logo and printed the notes on red paper. I pulled out the slick, black, imitation leather Bibles one by one and ran my fingers across the words *Holy Bible* stamped in gold on the cover. Then I haphazardly stuck my Christmas note in each one, wondering all the while what the likelihood was of the note being stuck in the exact page destined to personally inspire the guy who opened it.

I decided to sneak the Bibles into the locker room super late on Christmas Eve. I knew there was no chance anyone would be around at that time because Coach Carroll had given us three days off for the holiday. So, at about 11:00 p.m., I dragged the boxes back downstairs and loaded them into my car. The USC campus was usually buzzing with activity 24/7, but on Christmas Eve, it was like a ghost town. I used the yellowish glow of the campus lights to guide me as I drove in places that were technically off limits for cars, requiring some fancy maneuvering around metal barriers and a brief detour onto a sidewalk.

I parked and carried the boxes down the ramp one at a time and punched the code on the keypad. Since this was actually the basement of the building, it was nearly soundproof, and with the scant nighttime lighting, it was eerie and quiet. After carefully unpacking the Bibles and placing one on the seat in each locker, I felt the room fill with an undeniable holy presence, and I knew I wasn't alone. My heart cried out for the message on the pages of those books to bring hope to each of my teammates.

As I walked back up the ramp, I felt victorious. My spiritual journey of the last eight months was ending right here, right now. I had finally fulfilled my purpose, and my joy was overwhelming.

Throughout Christmas Day, my mind wasn't on presents or football or even pumpkin pie. All I could think about were those Bibles. My heart was brimming with hope and expectation. I could hardly wait for the next day to come.

On the morning of December 26, I pedaled over to the locker room, with the delirium of my excitement feeding some grandiose daydreams: maybe the entire team would be reading the Bibles when I walked through the door and then a revival of sorts might break out. The verse in Isaiah promised that the Word would not return empty, so while I didn't know exactly *what* was going to happen, I knew it was going to be something spectacular.

I took my time getting down to the locker room because I certainly did not want to be one of the first to arrive and arouse any suspicion of involvement with the mysterious gifts. When I entered the hallway, I heard some commotion so I knew there were guys already in the locker room. I nonchalantly strolled over to the door, acted like it was any other day, and punched in the code.

I took a deep breath, lifted my eyes, and slowly pulled the door open.

Still standing in the threshold, I could scarcely believe the sight that was before me. Everywhere I looked, shredded tissue-thin pages of the Bibles were strewn upon the floor, so much so that I could hardly see even a sliver of the cardinal carpet. I stood frozen in place as my heart sank and I felt the blood drain from my face.

Never in any of my daydreams had I envisioned a scene like this. While being cut from the team broke my ego and my injury broke me physically, this was a soul breaker. I stood there, not moving, as if my feet were stuck in buckets of concrete. I didn't know where to look. I didn't know what to think. I didn't know what to do.

Over the previous year, I had witnessed some of my teammates' wild buffoonery that would often snowball out of control. I had heard the tales of their parties. I had received a front-row seat to the stereotypical exploits of big-time college football players. But this? This seemed inconceivable and out of line, even for them.

Knowing that my cover would be blown if I didn't snap out of this stupor, I headed for my locker in a daze, crushing the pages of the Bibles beneath my feet. Along the way, I saw dozens of Bibles heaped in the trash can.

I noticed only one Bible remaining in its locker—mine.

I picked it up and shoved it to the back of the shelf in defeat. I couldn't even stand to look at it. It represented the utter failure the last eight months of my life had been as well as the end of all the hopes I had riding on finding my purpose on that team. On the way out to practice, I passed one other locker where the Bible had been placed on the shelf, but it gave me little consolation since I was almost positive the other ninety-eight were either on the floor or in the trash.

I trudged through the motions at practice, completely devoid of any emotion. I was dreading going back to the locker room because I couldn't bear to face it all over again. Sure enough, the locker room was exactly as I had left it, or maybe it was even worse. Now those hundreds of pristine pages were dirty and ripped and trampled all over the floor, an image that would be permanently seared on my heart.

WALK ON
When All Hope Seems Lost

Seeing those Bibles on the floor of the locker room was heart wrenching for me. I was so sure that gift would bring hope and joy to my teammates, and when that didn't happen, I hit one of the lowest points of my life. Think about a painful rejection or defeat you have experienced. How can you find hope in situations like that?

> Why, my soul, are you downcast?
>   Why so disturbed within me?
> Put your hope in God,
>   for I will yet praise him,
>   my Savior and my God.
>
> —Psalm 42:11, NIV

17

Comfort on the Casket

Every time I closed my eyes, that mishmash of torn white pages, scuffed black covers, and ripped red paper reappeared in my mind. But with preparations for the Rose Bowl in full swing, I made a conscious decision to figuratively wad up the disappointment from my failure, stuff it in the back of my locker, and focus all my energy on the week ahead.

Game day on January 1 was christened with picture-perfect weather, and as the buses drove into Pasadena and pulled up to Rose Bowl Stadium, I couldn't wait to get on the field. The Rose Bowl is the most majestic and stately, not to mention the oldest, of all the bowl stadiums. The thick, plush carpet of grass was a deep shade of emerald, and the contrast of the brilliant red Rose Bowl logo at mid-field was striking.

And to top it all off, the Rose Bowl served as the crown jewel in an unforgettable ten-month journey that had seen me face a serious shoulder injury, battle back from surgery, get in on one play to bring the "Get Ben In" campaign to fruition, and—for the most part—look, act, and feel like a certifiable football player. After all, I started as a scrawny 165-pound journalism student and had blossomed into a legit 195-pound walk-on wide receiver.

I went through warm-ups, Tyler and I played catch, and then we watched the team's eleven-on-eleven drills. Neither of us had ever participated in any of those plays, since they were considered the final tune-up for the starters, but I heard Sark bark in my direction, "Hey, Ben, we need a receiver, you're in at Z!"

Yanking my helmet on, I headed for the huddle while experiencing the same sheer panic as during the Notre Dame game when Sanchez called "I-right Victory on one" and I had no idea what my assignment was. I got to the huddle just in time to hear the quarterback make the play call. While I knew I was supposed to line up on the left side, I had absolutely no idea what to do when I got there. I frantically wracked my brain: *Z around, Z around, Z around . . . what the heck is Z around?*

Booty called out the snap count, and just as the ball passed from the center into the quarterback's waiting hands, it finally clicked: Z around was a reverse play where the Z receiver moved from left to right behind the line of scrimmage. *Phew!* I was incredibly relieved that I knew what to do and even more grateful that since I was merely a decoy, I wouldn't even be required to touch the ball.

Unfortunately, as I began my assignment, I mistimed my steps and ran smack dab into our starting running back, Chauncey Washington, bounced off him, and landed flat on my back with a *thud.* I was looking straight up through my facemask into that crystal-blue sky, but I got back on my feet as fast as possible, hoping no one would notice. I was at the Rose Bowl, the biggest game of my life, and had just accidentally slammed into our star running back, a player who would eventually be drafted by the Jacksonville Jaguars.

Apparently, Chauncey wasn't even aware of the collision. He moved through the play as if nothing had happened, perhaps thinking I was actually a defensive player attempting to tackle him. At first, no one said anything, but within a few minutes, guys were asking me if I was okay, and Sark laid into me, "Ben, what are you *doing?*"

Like a kid who had failed a test, I sheepishly apologized, "I'm so sorry, I didn't know that play." On my way back to the locker room, I noticed a bright-green grass stain on the front of my pristine white jersey over the right breastplate. *How in the world did that get there? I fell on my back!* I was so embarrassed. The Rose Bowl jersey is the one jersey you get to keep, and mine had a big grass stain on the front of it, from warm-ups no less!

We won the game against Michigan, 32–18, and the only phase that sputtered a little bit was our kicking game. Mario made two field goals and two extra points, but he also missed two extra points, which clearly upset him.

Instead of his ear-to-ear grin and nonstop joking, he sat on the bench with his head in his hands. I walked by a couple of times and offered him some encouragement—"You're good, you're good"— but it was difficult to watch him taking it so hard. I knew he was just having an off day and it wasn't a big deal.

After the Rose Bowl, we celebrated as a team on the field and in the locker room, and then we convened with family and friends for a big end-of-season party in a tent just outside the stadium. The next day, I flew home for a couple of days, which gave me some time to reflect on the football team experience. It had been filled with ups and downs and twists and turns—and took my breath away.

Yet I couldn't escape the reality that I didn't feel like I fulfilled a deeper purpose on the team. I still could not understand how I could have missed it after hearing that whisper on the steps: *I have a great purpose for you in this.* While it had been unmistakable at the time, God's whisper was now muffled, and I began to question if I ever heard it at all.

I returned to LA on January 5 for a fraternity retreat at Lake Arrowhead in the mountains of Southern California. We went to dinner at a Mexican restaurant and consumed a ridiculous amount of chips and salsa while watching the Dallas Cowboys battle the Seattle Seahawks in the NFL playoffs. I was still a big Cowboys fan, and since they hadn't won a playoff game in more than ten years, watching Dallas quarterback Tony Romo botch the hold for a short field goal attempt in the final seconds and hand the game to the Seahawks was heartbreaking.

I was completely unaware of how trivial that disenchantment was about to become.

I was alone in my room, replaying the Cowboy loss in my head, when my phone rang. I answered to hear a teammate's voice on the other end. My teammate didn't waste any time making small talk. He asked if I had heard about Mario.

I knew immediately what he was going to tell me: either Mario had decided to enter the NFL draft or had won another award.

"Mario died," he said instead.

My knees went weak. I sank to the side of the bed, unable to even comprehend what was happening. I groaned in disbelief. "No, no, no. What happened?"

"No one knows. He was found dead at the bottom of a cliff near his home in San Pedro." I ended the call and buried my face in the depths of my pillow as bellowing, gut-wrenching sobs racked my entire body.

I had never cried like that before.

It didn't take long before my uncontrollable bawling reached the ears of my fraternity brothers who were downstairs, and my friend Gen came up to investigate, "What's going on, Ben? Are you all right?" In between heaves I choked out the entire story.

The overwhelming grief was a convergence of so many emotions, but the most agonizing was the ache of unmistakable regret. *What if I had sat down next to him on the bench and encouraged him after those missed Rose Bowl kicks? What if I had made more of an effort to befriend him off the field? What if instead of anonymously leaving a Bible in his locker, I had shared my hope of heaven with him?*

Having never experienced the death of someone close to me, I was horrified at the finality of it all. I stayed in that prone position for hours. Every ounce of my strength drained away. I don't remember falling asleep, but I must have drifted off at some point. When I awoke the next morning, I was fully dressed in the exact same position. I felt as beat up as I had during those early weeks of practice and wondered if I could even lift my head off the pillow. But the heartache was much more painful than the muscle aches ever were. While I knew physical aches eventually faded, I was sure the pain in my heart would never heal.

On the morning of January 10, the entire team gathered at Heritage Hall dressed in dark suits. It was another sun-drenched, warm, beautiful California day, which was a decided contrast to the gloominess that engulfed us. We quietly loaded up on buses and headed toward Mario's funeral in San Pedro, just a few miles south of USC.

Even though the bus rides to the games were silent, there was always an underlying air of anticipation and excitement, but this suffocating silence was markedly different. We arrived at Mary Star of the Sea, a Catholic church in San Pedro, where the gridlock of traffic, along with the police barricades in this quiet neighborhood, looked eerily similar to the Coliseum on game day. There were thousands of people converging on the church. We filed off the bus and wordlessly entered the sanctuary.

We moved as one to the front of the church on the right side where ten wooden pews had been reserved for us. The pews were intended to hold ten regular-sized parishioners, but since most of the guys would count for two, we were stuffed in those pews so tightly that our shoulders were scrunched up to our ears.

I sat on the edge of that scarred wooden pew with my elbows on my knees and my head in my hands. Tears streamed down my face. Many of the pallbearers were our linemen, and they slowly moved down the center aisle with measured steps. The haunting tones of the pipe organ reverberated throughout the cavernous sanctuary. It was a heart-wrenching scene: those strapping young men just barely holding it together, straining under the weight of the casket. As they passed my aisle, I lifted my head just in time to see Mario's number 19 jersey spread across the top of the casket, along with an elaborate spray of red and gold roses and something else I never expected to see again. Centered atop that casket was a black book with a red piece of paper sticking out of it.

I recognized it immediately.

It was one of the Bibles I had placed in the lockers less than two weeks earlier. And in an instant, a wave of comfort washed over me. I had no idea what it meant, but I was thankful that the Bible was there, as if God was holding me in His arms during that grief-stricken time.

There were several speakers during the nearly two-hour service, including Mario's brother, Joey, and Coach Carroll, who gave the closing remarks. He talked about Mario with great affection and told how he never tired of hearing Mario's incredibly predictable response when he asked, "How ya doin'?" And with that infectious smile and ever-present twinkle in his eye, Mario would always reply, "Livin' the dream, Coach! Livin' the dream!" And by the time Coach Carroll was finished, he had the entire crowd on their feet, clapping and hooting and whistling and cheering for Mario as if he had just kicked a game-winning field goal in the Coliseum. But instead of the band striking up the USC fight song, the slow, steady tolling of the church bells signaled the conclusion of Mario's final game.

After the funeral, we quietly loaded back onto the buses for the drive to the cemetery. Since the buses could not maneuver through the meandering cemetery roads, they dropped us off, and we walked the rest of the way to the grave site.

I saw in the distance the shipyards of San Pedro with their enormous iron structures jutting into the horizon and, just beyond, the shimmering sea along with the outline of Catalina Island. It really was a beautiful setting, and from our vantage point we could see Mario's family seated under a canopy facing the casket and the gaping hole that would soon swallow up our teammate forever.

Because I hadn't attended a funeral since I was a young child, I had been filled with fear of the unknown and wondered how much sadness I would be able to bear. When we drove up to the church, the depth of my sorrow was beyond description, and I was shackled with grief. But once I saw the Bible on the casket, there was a definite shift in my spirit, and I was now able to partake in the celebration of Mario's love of life.

And by the time we walked back down to the entrance of the cemetery following the graveside service, I felt a blossom of hope, although I would not understand the genesis of it until several years later.

WALK ON
God's Comforting Touch

I experienced God's comforting touch when I looked up and saw the Bible on top of the casket at Mario's funeral that morning. In your pain, your sorrow, and your devastation, God is with you, reaching out with His personal touch and calling you to look up. No matter what you're facing right now, will you look up?

> The LORD is close to the brokenhearted;
> he rescues those whose spirits are
> crushed.
>
> **—Psalm 34:18**

18

Livin' the Dream

Nine men stood like statues on the line of scrimmage, awaiting the extra-point kick, while holder Michael McDonald knelt on the 10-yard line directly behind the long snapper. With everyone frozen in place, the seconds on the play clock ticked down, but that eleventh man was nowhere in sight, and a heavy silence blanketed the Coliseum as teary-eyed Trojan fans realized what was happening.

The placekicker wasn't coming.

Following a delay-of-game penalty, David Buehler ran onto the field and kicked the extra point, thus ending the moving "missing man" tribute by Coach Carroll and the Trojans in memory of their beloved Mario Danelo. It was August 30, the first game of the 2007 season, and remembrances of Mario were everywhere—in a pregame ceremony, stickers on the players' helmets, and a bright-yellow goalpost pad with number 19 and "Livin' the Dream" printed boldly in cardinal letters.

It had been more than six months since we said goodbye to Mario, but the pain of his death was still raw, especially for me. My life since Mario's funeral had been a whirlwind. In late February, I waited inside Goux's Gate to intercept Coach Carroll and thank him for my experience on the team. I hadn't seen him since the funeral, but his face lit up as he greeted me warmly: "Ben, what's up? Haven't seen you in a while." I expressed my gratitude for the incredible year and added, "I kind of feel indebted to you, and if there is anything I can do to give back, I would love to volunteer to help out."

He hesitated briefly before saying, "I've been thinking about something you may be perfect for." He told me that he would call in a couple of days to discuss it. I thought it was cool that there might be some way for me to help out, but I was completely unprepared for what he was about to propose.

When I answered his phone call a few days later, he was talking a million miles a minute, and I caught only snatches of words and phrases here and there. "USC *Ripsit* website . . . recruiting thing . . . tell the story of the team . . . show people what it's like on the inside." None of it made any sense to me. I had no idea what he was trying to communicate and was completely lost when he wrapped up the call by saying, "I don't really know anything about websites, but maybe you do, and you can write it and run it and do what you do."

Quite bewildered, I said, "Wait, what?" I asked him to slow down and repeat everything. So he launched in again, and as his words and thoughts tumbled out, I was trying to decide if I should tell him that I did not know anything about creating a website. I was a reporter and a decent writer, but webmaster? I didn't want to put myself out of the running for the project, so I optimistically responded, "Coach, I'm not the best with web stuff, but I can learn and I can write." He closed the conversation with "Yeah, you are good at writing, so I think you should give it a try." The whole thing sounded a little wacky, but I was honored that he had confidence in me, so I decided to give it a shot.

He told me to "brainstorm and get some ideas on paper," and I typed up a page of thoughts. When I presented it to him, I hesitantly asked, "Is that what you are looking for?" Judging by the confused look on his face, I realized what a really silly question that was, as *he* had no earthly idea what he was looking for.

So I signed on to create something that had never been done before with a guy who couldn't really tell me what it was supposed to look like. It was classic Coach Carroll when it came to nonfootball matters: brimming with visionary ideas, yet a bit fuzzy on the nitty-gritty details of execution. He asked me to present my ideas to the coaching staff, which was the most intimidating thing I had ever done. I felt terrified facing all my former coaches, especially Sark, whose skepticism about my football skills had now been surpassed by his skepticism about my webmaster skills. Lucky for me, though, as little as I knew about the whole thing, they knew even less, and the entire presentation went right over their heads.

Coach Carroll hired me the next day on an experimental basis at ten dollars an hour for the summer and said if the project went well, he would offer me a full-time job. As my grad school graduation was still four months away and I hadn't put much effort into looking for a job yet, I jumped at the opportunity and set forth to make the most of it.

My first "office" was the same reception area where I spent all those hours perched on the couch when I was injured. A coffee table became my desk and was completely covered with my notes and scribbled drawings along with my yellow pad, my flip phone, and my laptop. People paraded in and out of "my office" all day long, probably wondering exactly what I was doing there.

As the days slipped by, the result of my efforts was the creation of a brand-new site called USC *Ripsit,* and I kept pushing Coach Carroll about the full-time job. I was technically still in school finishing my master's thesis for my communication management degree, but I knew I couldn't make it in LA on ten dollars an hour. So three days before training camp, he offered me a full-time position with a raise to eighteen dollars per hour and a significant upgrade in terms of my office. I started sharing a desk with Morgon, his executive assistant. Apparently, Morgon wasn't thrilled with looking across her desk at me all day long, so she suggested we convert a cherrywood armoire in the corner of her office into my desk. It stood about six feet tall and had two doors that swung open to reveal a clothes rack, a shelf, and a couple of drawers. We removed the clothes rack and the drawers and adjusted the shelf to a desk height. My knees bumped into the back of the armoire, and though it wasn't perfect, the location was prime real estate since it was right outside Coach Carroll's office.

For the next three years, I had a blast bringing USC *Ripsit* to life and giving our fans unprecedented access to Coach Carroll and the Trojans through the newfound world of social media. What began as another one of Coach Carroll's wild ideas was rapidly becoming the envy of sports teams across the country. Our website was the definitive news source for USC football, featuring everything from team meeting photos to injury updates to what song Coach Carroll was currently jamming to in his office.

We were pioneers in a new era of sports media, and Coach Carroll became so invested in the project that we fed off each other, sharing new ideas every time he walked by. We just kept tossing thoughts out like a wad of spaghetti noodles to see what would stick. And crazily, most of it did. Our page view statistics were off the charts. CNBC even named it the best all-access blog in sports.

New-fangled Facebook and Twitter became our next frontiers, and the success was nearly instantaneous. Coach Carroll's personal Facebook page maxed out on friends within minutes, and Twitter followed the same meteoric trajectory as he gained more than a hundred thousand followers in his first few months on the burgeoning social media site. He was even hailed as "the Facebook Coach" by one publication for going where no coach had gone before.

I had a little digital camera I took everywhere to document those behind-the-scenes moments we highlighted on the website's signature feature, the *Ripsit* blog. Some pictures were fairly mundane: the players checking into the dorms before training camp, for example, or a photo from an empty training room. But often I was just in the right place at the right time when something magical happened.

So it was during the first week of fall camp in 2009 when an impromptu talent show took place during a team meeting. The guys started pushing one of the freshman, Marquis Simmons, to get up and sing. He was clearly embarrassed, so the first lines were quiet and hesitant, as he nervously chuckled into his palm. But as his confidence increased, so did his intensity, and we were all blown away as this rich, deep, melodious voice filled the room with strains of Bill Withers's "Lean on Me." It wasn't long before the entire team was clapping and yelling as they rose to their feet, arms around one another's shoulders, belting out the lyrics.

The whole thing was over in a minute, but I captured it on video. This was before the widespread use of smartphones, and it was a

Friday night, when most people planned to do something more exciting than sitting in front of their computers. Even so, we posted the fifty-second video on the blog right after the meeting, and it went viral overnight. The next morning, a barrage of requests from media outlets filled my inbox, including one from *SportsCenter* asking for permission to run the video.

As cool as that was, it went to a whole new level when Coach Carroll invited Bill Withers, the singer-songwriter who wrote and recorded "Lean on Me," to make a surprise appearance at a team meeting. Of course, Coach Carroll couldn't do something ordinary like just introduce the guy. Instead, thanks to Bill's creative idea, Coach shared a lengthy and solemn story about how we were being investigated for mold growing in our showers and said Bill was the NCAA inspector. Playing his role to perfection, Bill and his theatrical assistant (his daughter Kori) launched into a drawn-out explanation of the special knee-high shower shoes the players would soon be required to wear. The room was deathly quiet, guys listening in disbelief and hanging on his every word, when Bill wryly smiled and said, "You've been punked!" The room erupted in laughter and applause.

Bill told the guys how much it meant to him that they enjoyed his song and said he had a simple request: for Marquis to sing his song one more time. As if singing in front of the guys wasn't nerve-racking enough, this was almost too much for poor Marquis. It took some special encouragement from Bill to get him singing again, and when everyone chimed in, "You just call on me, brother, when you need a hand," it was a once-in-a-lifetime moment that none of us would ever forget. This time, we set aside my dinky camera and captured it all with the help of our professional video staff. We posted the clip immediately, and it too was an overnight sensation, twice as popular as the first one.

With my creativity unleashed on a blank canvas and an environment where I had no fear of failure, I was thriving. My journalism skills, coupled with my insatiable desire to harness the power of this emerging technology, made every day an adventure. And Coach Carroll's philosophy of doing things better than they had ever been done before was being surpassed by the reality that we were doing things that had *never* been done before. Somewhere along the way, he and I began to develop this unique partnership, a mind meld of sorts, where we often came up with a similar idea at the same time, and I was growing to appreciate him in a whole new way.

I thought he was on his way to becoming the college football version of UCLA's ten-time championship-winning basketball coach John Wooden, building upon his storied career and staying at USC until retirement. And I would become an adjunct professor in the journalism department, with dreams of moving on to serve as the athletic director one day.

That's why the breaking news on *SportsCenter* on January 5 blindsided me.

Coach Carroll was considering an offer from the Seattle Seahawks. When I heard the news, my heart just dropped. I felt sad, angry, and somewhat betrayed. All my friends were calling to see what was going on. They assumed, of course, that I would know what was happening. I mean, how could I not know? I was practically his right-hand man. *Why didn't he tell me? I thought we were going to be working together forever.*

He called me later that morning when I was sitting in my car in a grocery store parking lot and said, "Hey, I wish I could have told you, but I couldn't tell anyone because I had to keep it under wraps." I didn't respond so he charged on excitedly, "I haven't taken the job yet, and I'm still weighing all my options." Then he asked, "What do you think I should do?"

My disappointment spilled over when I replied, "Congrats on the offer. To be honest, I kind of feel jilted because I thought you were going to stay at USC forever." I added, "I just don't really know what to think about it."

He pressed me, "Do you think I should take it?"

So here's the top college football coach in the country asking twenty-four-year-old me for my opinion on his career choice, and since I was still ticked off, I said, "Don't do what I think."

"Well, Ben, what do you think?"

After a deep breath, I replied, "I think you should stay at USC."

I knew full well he wasn't going to make his decision based on my recommendation; he was just trying to make me feel part of it. I wasn't a bit surprised when later that day the news broke confirming he had accepted the position and was heading to the Seahawks. He called the next day to tell me he wanted me to join him as soon as he filled a slew of open positions and got everything lined up. He held a press conference in Seattle the following day, I packed up his office at USC, and just like that, he was gone.

Lane Kiffin was coaching for the University of Tennessee at the time and was hired as USC's new head coach almost immediately. Our paths were about to cross again, and I knew that didn't bode well for me in my role as director of online media. He never seemed to like me as a player, and upon his arrival, he seemed to have no interest in USC *Ripsit* or any of the other projects I had put together with Coach Carroll. I tried to explain the benefits of what we were doing, but he just didn't seem to see any value in it—or in me.

For the next two months, while I continued to work at USC, Coach Carroll called me every Wednesday night and told me he was getting closer to bringing me to Seattle. I really wanted to stay in Southern California because that's where all my friends were, but my frustration working for a new coach who didn't share my vision was making Seattle look a whole lot sunnier. (Down the road, Kiff and I developed a friendship and a great appreciation for each other.)

I finally decided that I couldn't wait around any longer for Coach Carroll to sort out his staff issues. I was growing more miserable by the minute, and I didn't even really know if he was being serious or just being nice. I started actively looking for a new job that would allow me to stay in Southern California. When an opportunity arose with the San Diego Chargers, I jumped on it. I was invited to their offices for an interview, and as I drove back to LA, they called and offered me the job. Although I was 99 percent positive I was going to accept it, I told them I wanted to sleep on it.

I decided to text Coach Carroll to share the news. I typed out a brief message that read, "Hey Coach, thanks so much for everything over the years. I'm taking a job with the Chargers in their media department so hopefully I'll see you on the field this fall." I hit the Send button and almost instantly my phone started ringing. When I answered, he emphatically said, "You cannot take that job. I have a job up here for you. We are going to make it happen." His voice took on a note of urgency. "You need to get on a plane as soon as possible because we need you up here."

And within days I was stepping off a plane at Seattle-Tacoma International Airport on a rainy, cold night. I checked in at the hotel and had to walk what seemed like miles to find a Subway that was still open. My sweatshirt was soaked through, my teeth were chattering, and I was freezing. I wished I had packed a raincoat, but the problem wasn't that I had forgotten my raincoat. The problem was that I didn't own one. And I thought to myself, *Why would anyone ever want to live here? This is absolutely miserable.*

I was ushered into Coach Carroll's office the next morning, and he was just as chipper and happy as ever when he exclaimed, "Ben, I've been missing your smiling face all these months." And before he blinked, I knew I was meant to be there. The band was back together. Within two weeks, I packed up everything I owned and moved to Seattle, completely confident that was where God wanted me.

I had no clue that my greatest joy there would not be found in being back with Coach Carroll or even in a diamond-studded Super Bowl ring. An old friend was about to reenter my life and tell me an utterly amazing story that I would hardly believe.

WALK ON
Faith in God's Timing

I thought Coach Carroll would be a Trojan until he retired, and I figured I would go on to a successful career at USC. Even though we all have hopes for our lives, they pale in comparison to the dreams God has for us. They are far greater than anything we could fathom. How can you live trustingly one day at a time, placing your faith in His perfect ways and flawless timing?

> "My thoughts are nothing like your thoughts,"
>   says the LORD. "And my ways are far beyond
>   anything you could imagine.
> For just as the heavens are higher than the earth,
>   so my ways are higher than your ways
>   and my thoughts higher than your thoughts."
>
> —Isaiah 55:8-9

19

Utterly Amazed

Transitioning from eight years of being in my tight-knit USC community of college buddies to a city where I knew no one except Coach Carroll plunged me abruptly into what is known as the Seattle Freeze, a commonly held belief that it is very difficult for transplants to make friends with Seattleites. I was so lonely, I worked twelve-hour days just so I didn't have to go home to an empty apartment. I visited a new church every Sunday, sitting by myself while mentally reciting the same prayer: *Lord, please let me sit next to some nice person who will invite me to lunch.*

But after a month, I struggled to make even one friend.

In May an old USC buddy came to visit, and feeling sorry for my predicament, he connected me with a friend of a friend named Char Beck. It was extremely difficult for me to reach out to someone I didn't know since I was such an introvert, but I was getting desperate, so I sent Char a Facebook message. Surprisingly, he answered within minutes and offered to meet me for dinner. We started getting together regularly, and although he was my polar opposite, with his super-extroverted, larger-than-life personality, I loved spending time with him and dared to hope that I had found my first friend in Seattle.

Char told me about a Christian mentorship program for high school students called Young Life and suggested I check it out. I had never heard of it before, but I thought if I could make more friends like Char there, it was definitely worth a try. I met Marshall Jamieson, the Young Life area director on Mercer Island, and he invited me to an informational meeting for volunteers a week later in his home.

The group at Marshall's home was very welcoming. All the volunteers seemed to really enjoy being together, like one big, happy family. As everyone was arriving and chatting, I told Marshall's wife, Emily, about my background at USC, and she excitedly said, "You were at USC? And you played football? My brother was on the team there! Taylor Odegard. Do you know him?"

"Taylor? Taylor Odegard? No way!" I replied. A picture of Taylor and Mario goofing around on the sideline during practice filled my mind.

She rambled on about what a small world it was, how much she enjoyed USC football and loved Coach Carroll. Her last comment flabbergasted me. "Taylor is going to start volunteering with Young Life too, so you'll probably see him tonight."

The Taylor Odegard I knew at USC was the stereotypical jock who seemed to party hard and have a string of girls on each arm. He was one of the punters the year I was on the team, and while I wasn't close to him, I knew he was tight with Mario since he was his holder. A placekicker and his holder have a unique relationship that is forged in the 1.5 seconds it takes to launch the ball from the lightning-fast hands of the long snapper to the steady, poised palms of the holder who is trusted to position it perfectly for the kicker. Perhaps even more important is the holder's emotional support. His words of encouragement are the last words the kicker hears before the kick, and his words of congratulations or solace are the first words the kicker hears after the kick. The relationship between a placekicker and his holder is considered sacred.

Placekickers are somewhat outcasts during practice since they are exempt from many of the drills and reps for the rest of the team. It's up to them to carve out their own place among their teammates. If the kicker acts like a prima donna or doesn't attempt to engage with the rest of the guys, he may soon be ostracized. But Mario and Taylor went out of their way to make sure that didn't happen.

They attended the early morning conditioning sessions to run and lift with the linemen, which earned them a tremendous amount of respect. And since they had a lot of free time during practice, they were always joking around with us and razzing the coaches by tripping them and talking smack to Sark and Kiff at every opportunity. They became known as the unofficial mayors of the team. Taylor and Mario shared a bond that made them as close as brothers, both on and off the field.

What in the world would Taylor be doing at a Christian organization like Young Life? I wondered. Marshall had insisted upon meeting me in advance to make sure I had the depth of faith and strength of character to lead these high school guys. *Did Emily even know what her brother was like in college?*

My thoughts were interrupted when the front door opened and Taylor was standing at the threshold. He stopped in his tracks, eyes wide in surprise as he tried to process seeing me in a completely unexpected setting. After a quick greeting of "Malcolmson, what are you doing here?" we stepped out through the sliding glass door into the backyard and wrapped each other in a big hug. It had been more than three years since we had last been together—at Mario's funeral.

We spent the next few minutes catching up, and he must have sensed I was having trouble understanding why he would be interested in an organization like Young Life. His tone changed, and he got a very serious look on his face. "Dude, my life has totally turned around in the past few years." He proceeded to tell me that he had grown up on Mercer Island in a Christian home but had drifted away during college, wanting to live life on his own terms. But at the end of the 2006 season, God intervened and altered the course of Taylor's life forever.

"Do you remember the last week we were on the team and someone put all those Bibles in our lockers?" Taylor asked me.

My mouth went dry as the sting of embarrassment and the painful rejection of that day came flooding back. I froze. Trying to mask my emotions, I told myself, *Play dumb. Play dumb. Play dumb.* I wasn't sure whether I should burst into laughter or weep. I muttered, "Yeah, I think I kind of remember that."

"When I saw all those Bibles trashed on the floor, I was sick to my stomach," he began. Even though, as Taylor said, his "life had gotten in the way of Jesus" during college, he valued the words on those tattered pages and thought it was shameful for his teammates to treat that gift so irreverently.

"I was running late and in a hurry to get on the field that morning," Taylor continued, "especially since I knew how strict Coach Carlisle was about being on time for practice." While Carlisle was an incredible strength and conditioning coach and a great guy, he got hard-nosed if you were late, and we'd all witnessed the punishment meted out to offenders: bear crawls on the treadmill until you couldn't walk.

"As I was pushing the door open and racing out to practice," Taylor went on, "I heard a familiar voice from somewhere behind me in the locker room asking, 'Does anyone know how to read this thing?' I was already halfway out the door and torn between wanting to respond to a teammate and not daring to be late to practice."

As badly as he wanted to ignore the voice, Taylor said he felt an undeniable nudge to close the door and stop. He walked back around the corner and saw his best friend, Mario, sitting in his locker in half pads with one of the Bibles on his lap. Mario had a sincerely perplexed look on his face as he asked, "What is this thing? How do you read it?"

Taylor chuckled as he said, "What do you mean?"

Mario replied, "How do you read this thing? Do you read it like a book or what?"

At first Taylor thought Mario was joking, but after a couple of seconds, he realized his friend was serious and whispered a quick prayer, "Jesus, give me the words," as he set his pads on the floor and sat next to Mario. It had been years since Taylor had shared his faith with anyone, but with seeds of truth having been planted in his heart since childhood, the truth came pouring out. And for the next forty-five minutes, Taylor told Mario about Jesus and how He came to give us a relationship with God and make us right with Him.

Taylor knew Mario liked to understand how things worked, so he shared a big-picture overview, explaining a bit of the history of the Old and New Testaments. When Mario asked where he should start reading, Taylor suggested the Gospels, since Matthew, Mark, Luke, and John were Jesus's "boys" who made up His "team." He explained how he could identify the words of Jesus since they were printed in red. Taylor said he prayed with Mario before heading out to practice that he might have an open heart to hear the voice of God.

As Taylor recounted this story, I felt a confluence of feelings somewhat akin to the day I found out I made the team: shock, wonder, disbelief. I could hear the shredded pages crinkling beneath my feet on the locker room floor, see the scuffed black covers piled high in the trash can, and still taste the bitterness of my doubt. As my mind battled my heart, I remembered the sweet sound of the whisper on the steps: *I have a great purpose for you in this.*

What if I hadn't missed my purpose after all? And then, my shock turned to awe. *Can this be real?*

Taylor went on to describe a transformation in Mario over the days leading up to the Rose Bowl. The special teams guys, and especially the kickers, were notorious for horsing around while they waited for team meetings to start, and typically Mario would be at the center of the action, cracking jokes and stirring things up. But Taylor said that for the next six days, Mario was noticeably absent from his usual shenanigans because he was sitting in his locker, reading his Bible during every free moment or asking Taylor questions about God, Jesus, the Bible, and everything in between. Taylor described it as Mario's insatiable thirst to drink in the truth on those pages and unlock its mysteries in a way he had never done before. Mario met God in a new, real, and profound way, and it was apparent in the manner he lived the final days of his life.

As if sensing my wonder, Taylor paused and said, smiling, "Isn't that a crazy story?"

I choked out, "Yeah, it's the craziest story I've ever heard. And it's even crazier because I was the one who put those Bibles in the lockers, and I thought it was a total failure."

Taylor was speechless. For me, there were also no words. It was as if I had been ushered straight into God's presence.

We hugged each other fiercely and struggled to keep our tears at bay. When Taylor found his voice again, he told me that Mario's death had broken him completely. Did he share enough of his faith in Jesus? Did he say the right things? Could he have done more? Taylor said he would never forget seeing that Bible on top of the casket at the funeral, the same Bible that he and Mario read together a few days earlier.

It was ultimately some comforting words from Taylor's dad that finally healed his hurting heart. "In many, many years when you get to heaven, you will hear, 'Well done, my good and faithful servant,'" his dad told him. "And as Mario walks toward you, wearing his 'livin' the dream' grin, he'll be saying, 'Good to see you, Odegard. That was the best hold you ever gave me.'"

Taylor walked back inside and left me alone. I closed my eyes and was transported back to that wooden pew during Mario's funeral at Mary Star of the Sea. But this time, when I lifted my head and focused through my tear-filled eyes on the Bible, I understood what God had been saying to me that day: *I got you, Ben. I got you.* Time stood still, and in the eyes of my heart that Bible turned into a crown.

An immeasurable peace enveloped me as God spoke softly into my soul, *Mario is with Me.*

And that whisper on the steps became a triumphant shout of joy. *I did have a great purpose for you in this.*

WALK ON
Be Utterly Amazed

Even when your life reaches its bleakest point and you face seemingly insurmountable circumstances, God has plans for you that you would not believe, even if He told you. He took a skinny student newspaper reporter who hadn't played football since the fifth grade and placed him on the nation's top-ranked college football team, only to get seriously injured, battle back through rehab, get in for one play, aim to find a God-given purpose, struggle with the death of a teammate, and eventually discover four years later the fulfillment of an utterly amazing calling. Are you prepared to be utterly amazed and walk on in faith, expecting God to do something in your days that you would not believe, even if you were told?

> Look at the nations and watch—
>   and be utterly amazed.
> For I am going to do something in your days
>   that you would not believe,
>   even if you were told.
>
> **—Habakkuk 1:5, NIV**

CONCLUSION

The Nudge

Deafening. That's one way to describe the noise on the sideline during a Seahawks home game. When the 12s (the affectionate term for our fans) take over CenturyLink Field, saying they are loud is like saying Usain Bolt is fast. According to *Guinness World Records 2013,* their reverberating ruckus in September 2013 measured 137.6 decibels, which is almost as loud as the noise of a military jet taking off from an aircraft carrier. (At 150 decibels your eardrums rupture!)

When you combine that kind of noise with your eye-level angle of the action, speed, and complexity of every NFL matchup, you simply can't be aware of everything that is going on during the game. That's why the day following every game, Coach Carroll leads our "Tell the Truth" meetings, and every member of our team is challenged to deal with the facts of the game he just played, both the positives and the negatives, in an open and honest way.

What I've learned from sitting in on those meetings for the past eleven-plus years is that the real truth seekers gain a new perspective, one that allows them to answer the "why" questions of the game. They're questions like "Why did I win that route?" or "Why did they sack our quarterback?" or "Why did we score a touchdown on that play?"

Deafening. That's also how I would describe what goes on in my noisy life filled with work and traffic and emails and chores and bills and social media and family responsibilities and, and, and—you can probably name a hundred noisemakers in your life. In much the same way that the coaches and players have to wait until after game day to see how everything unfolded and address those all-important "why" questions, you and I face a similar dilemma. We simply cannot answer the "why" questions of life amidst the daily racket that bombards us. Oftentimes we have to wait months or years to be able to answer those questions: "Why did I lose my job?" or "Why do I struggle with anxiety?" or "Why did God allow this pain to happen?"

Now that more than ten years have passed since I suited up as a Trojan, I can look back with that same invaluable postgame perspective and see how God used my circumstances to build me into the man He wanted me to be.

Hopeful. There was no way I could have anticipated the phone call from Lana on the day I made the team or the one from Coach Carroll inviting me to join the Seahawks organization as his special assistant. Believe me, there are plenty of days when nothing extraordinary happens at the Seahawks headquarters: I coordinate a meeting, plan a public appearance for Coach, entertain a guest at practice, or perform one of a thousand other seemingly menial tasks. But because I never know what God might surprise me with, I aim to approach each day with a hopeful expectation that He has a great purpose for my life.

Confident. Thinking back to those times God filled me with a courage I wouldn't normally possess bolsters my confidence to be brave. Going through the tryouts for the number one football team in the country with essentially no football experience was one of the scariest things I have ever done. But seeing how God worked in my life after I acted upon that nudge gives me courage to step out again and again. It's still tough for me. In fact, with my introverted personality and fear of failure, it isn't that much easier for me today than it was the day I timidly introduced myself to Coach Carroll after covering my first practice as a student newspaper reporter. Nowadays, I draw upon that courage every time I have a difficult conversation with Coach, challenging him on a decision or presenting a new and outlandish project idea to him. It's all with the intent of helping him be in the best position to succeed, but it doesn't lessen the sting of potential rejection or pushback in those moments.

Encouraging. The indelible impression Deerfoot made on my life prompted me to become a mentor for a crew of young men through the faith-based Young Life program on Mercer Island, the same group where I reconnected with Taylor on his sister's patio in 2010. Some of the games I now treasure the most are not those I watched standing on an NFL sideline but games I saw sitting in the stands at Mercer Island High School cheering for my guys. And I'm always thrilled when my vacation time includes a trip to Malibu Club, Young Life's camp in British Columbia, where many students experience the best week of their lives. Watching my guys meet God in the middle of that Canadian wilderness and seeing their desire to go deeper in their faith fueled, just as I experienced at Deerfoot, is always one of the highlights of my year.

Intentional. As sports editor, I relied on my own strength and let myself get swallowed up by my job responsibilities. I didn't carve out the time to strengthen my faith and become the man God wanted me to be. In the fast-paced world of the NFL, it would be very easy for me to slip back into that old pattern. The demands of my job are innumerable—everything from helping Coach Carroll formulate his thoughts for a team meeting to managing his external communication to hosting famous dignitaries, movie stars, and rappers—all while facing ridiculously tight deadlines. Over the years, I have become intentional about creating space in my schedule to spend time with other believers and stay connected to community, no matter how hectic my schedule gets.

Dependent. Remember when I interned at the *Dallas Morning News* and built time into my evenings for prayer walks? Or turned the radio off in my car so I could pray while I was driving to my assignments? Those are practices I still employ today. Every morning when I drive to work across the I-90 bridge, I turn the music off and contemplate my day while I pray for God to use me in my role and in my relationships at the Seahawks. And oftentimes when I am in the midst of a chaotic day, I slip out to walk around our indoor field to pray, listen for God's direction, and respond to any nudges I am feeling on my heart.

Trusting. I can still taste the bitter disappointments I experienced with the fraternity house, my injury, and the apparent failure of my team Bible study and prayer group and the Bibles in the lockers, moments when I had acted on what I wholeheartedly believed was a nudge from God. Yet it felt as if He may have abandoned me and forgotten His promise of purpose. In every one of those situations, God taught me to wait on Him and trust Him with my unfulfilled desires and deepest hurts. Today, there are still areas in my life where I struggle with disappointment in seeing my purpose not come to fruition. I long for many of my family members, friends, and coworkers to trust God more with their lives and share in this adventure of faith. When I get discouraged or impatient, I remember all those times He was working behind the scenes in my life, which inspires me to continue listening for and responding to those nudges.

Two thousand years ago, a man named Peter responded to a nudge of his own. While he was in a boat in the middle of a lake, his friend Jesus walked on the water and invited Peter to join him (see Matthew 14).

"Take courage!" the Son of God said to His friend. "It is I. Don't be afraid."

Peter, clearly startled, said to Jesus, "Lord, if it's You, tell me to come to You on the water."

"Come," Jesus said, nudging Peter on. And in that moment, Peter chose courage over fear as he stepped out of his boat to walk on the water, moving toward Jesus—and embracing a once-in-a-lifetime opportunity to walk on in his faith and impact the lives of people around him.

It's quite possible God has used my story to give you a nudge that can help you walk on in your faith and impact the people around you. I sincerely hope He has.

Where do you see yourself in my story? Maybe you connect with Mario, and you do not know much about Jesus or have never really considered the role of God in your life. Or perhaps you identify with Taylor: you have a faith background but have been living life on your own terms lately. Or maybe you see yourself in me, and you desire to see your God-given purpose come to life but you're facing defeat and discouragement.

What is the nudge you're feeling right now?

If you're similar to Mario, maybe that nudge is to open your heart to Jesus, the way Mario opened up his Bible that December morning a week before he passed away. If you connect with Taylor, that nudge could be to set down your old life and turn to Jesus, as Taylor set down his pads and responded to God's nudge in the locker room that day. Or if you click with me, your nudge might be to remain faithful to Jesus as you continue to seek your God-given purpose, trusting that He is at work in your life in whatever metaphorical locker room you find yourself in.

The greatest benefit of every postgame breakdown is the hindsight perspective that's simply impossible to achieve in the heat of the moment. In the midst of a game, we can never anticipate which play will be the game changer: the fumble that is returned for a touchdown, the goal-line stand, or the scramble by the quarterback for the first down.

The same is true in life. I had no idea that the phone call or the tryout or my stint as sports editor would alter the trajectory of my life forever. We never know which situation God will use as a life changer.

But while we can't anticipate when those life-changer moments will appear, we can have the confidence that God is nudging us along, whispering, *Walk on, dear child, walk on. I have a great purpose for you in this.*

Whether you turn to the right or to the left,
your ears will hear a voice behind you,
saying, "This is the way; walk in it."

—Isaiah 30:21, NIV

Acknowledgments

Just like football, writing this book was the ultimate team sport, and so many people played significant roles during the two-and-a-half-year process. This team is stacked with MVPs, and I'm incredibly blessed each of them was willing to lace up a pair of cleats and get in the game. It's my honor to introduce them to you as they run out of the tunnel.

Quarterback: First and foremost, our franchise player from day one has been Patti McCord, the multitalented, forever-passionate, do-it-all writer who took a leap of faith to call me out of the blue in January 2016 to encourage me to write this book. Over the next twenty-four months, we wrote a book and, most importantly, I gained a dear friend. Simply put, this book would not exist without Patti, a winsome world changer who provided endless amounts of encouragement, dedication, creativity, care, and joy to this project from start to finish. She's a true superstar. I'm forever grateful for Patti and her passion to see this book blossom into the best it could possibly be.

Head Coaches: My editors, Shannon Marchese and Andrew Stoddard, who were willing to take a chance on this ragtag unproven rookie. Their patience and encouragement, along with some outstanding play calls and leadership along the way, were top caliber. And special thanks goes to Laura Wright, our phenomenal production editor, who patiently provided her expertise to get this book into the end zone.

Kickoff Specialists: Randy Guista, who did not hesitate when asked to suit up and made the initial connection between Patti and me, and Maria Goff, whose encouragement launched my story off the tee. From the start, Randy and Maria stirred up a sense of "watch what God will do" that carried us through to the end.

Assistant Coaches: Dr. Dean Nelson, Donald Miller, and Ryan Holiday, each of whom believed in my story from the very beginning and generously offered guidance, support, and encouragement along the way.

Wide Receivers: Rolf Benirschke, Bob Schrimpf, and Rick Parker, who graciously shared their time and expertise. Also, utmost gratitude goes out to Taylor Odegard and Mike Escoto, who were at the heart of my story ten years ago and readily agreed to jump back into the game when reviewing the events.

Running Back: The wonderful Traci Grant, who was our workhorse on the ground in the early part of the game. Without her unselfish sacrifice to power through nearly one hundred thousand words and offer her editing expertise and advice, I would most likely still be in the locker room.

Offensive Line: All those who stood their ground to give valuable input and hold off the discouragement and doubt when the scoreboard wasn't tipped in our favor during the disheartening days of the writing process: Vince Grant; Greg, Jana, and Wes McCord; and Amanda Woodruff.

Players Coming off the Bench: All those friends and family members who were praying fervently and cheering wholeheartedly throughout the journey: Doug and Debbie Ament; Julz Arney; Char Beck; Candice Brooks; Kelly Creeden; Jill Flyckt; Kathy Franklin; Carly, Emilie, and Cole Grant; Rick and Michele Hamada; Garrett Hanson; Chris Herring; Steve Hougard; Marshall and Emily Jamieson; Gary Klein; David Kroll; Preston Langholz; Sydel McKim; Sam Mean; Lee Merry; my beautiful bride, Brittney Malcolmson; Clay Malcolmson; Ken and Stacey Malcolmson; Marti Parker; Collin Roberts; Katie Rusk; Roy and Rose Sandstrom; Judah Smith; Ed Smyth; Dixie Stanforth; Michael Stead; Jake Stenberg; Ryan Swedberg; and Gary Uberstine.

And of course, **Pete Carroll,** the person who has played the single most significant role in this story and in my life.

Above all, none of this would have been possible without our **Lord and Savior Jesus Christ,** who wrote this story before time began and gives us all a purpose that we cannot fathom. "Now to him who is able to do immeasurably more than all we ask or imagine, according to his power that is at work within us, to him be glory in the church and in Christ Jesus throughout all generations, for ever and ever! Amen" (Ephesians 3:20–21, NIV).

Connect with the Author

After a story like this one, perhaps you're wondering, *Could something like that happen to me?*

Yes! And immeasurably more!

As you walk on in courageous hope and take those small steps of faithful obedience, I'm confident God has something utterly amazing and miraculous for your life too. And when that happens, I'd love to hear about how God connects *your* story to *my* story.

I am blessed every time I get the opportunity to share my story in person with churches, youth groups, and corporate audiences across the country. So if you'd like to share your story or invite me to speak to your group, I'd love to hear from you:

Website: BenMalcolmson.com
Email: Ben@BenMalcolmson.com
Instagram: @BenMalcolmson
Twitter: @BenMalcolmson
Facebook: @BenMalcolmsonBook